# BUILDING ELEMENTARY READING SKILLS
# THROUGH WHOLE LANGUAGE AND LITERATURE

# BUILDING ELEMENTARY READING SKILLS THROUGH WHOLE LANGUAGE AND LITERATURE

*By*

## DONALD C. CUSHENBERY, ED.D.

*Professor of Education*
*University of Nebraska at Omaha*
*Omaha, Nebraska*

CHARLES C THOMAS • PUBLISHER
*Springfield • Illinois • U.S.A.*

*Published and Distributed Throughout the World by*

CHARLES C THOMAS • PUBLISHER
2600 South First Street
Springfield, Illinois 62794-9265

© *1989 by* CHARLES C THOMAS • PUBLISHER
ISBN 0-398-05626-9
Library of Congress Catalog Card Number: 89-36759

*With* THOMAS BOOKS *careful attention is given to all details of manufacturing
and design. It is the Publisher's desire to present books that are satisfactory as to their
physical qualities and artistic possibilities and appropriate for their particular use.*
THOMAS BOOKS *will be true to those laws of quality that assure a good name
and good will.*

*Printed in the United States of America*
*SC-R-3*

**Library of Congress Cataloging-in-Publication Data**

Cushenbery, Donald C.
  Building elementary reading skills through whole language and
literature / by Donald C. Cushenbery.
    p.   cm.
  Includes bibliographical references.
  ISBN 0-398-05626-9
  1. Reading (Elementary)—Language experience approach.   I. Title.
LB1573.33.C87   1989
372.4'14—dc20                                                   89-36759
                                                                 CIP

*To my wife, Rita,*
*an outstanding elementary teacher*
*for many years*

# PREFACE

At the present time, the status of elementary reading instructional procedures is undergoing a definitive change *from* the teaching of hundreds of discrete reading subskills *to* a new and more productive curriculum that emphasizes the whole language approach. Many noted reading specialists have come to the inescapable conclusion that the subskill methods promoted the memorization of a myriad of reading principles without adequate practice in combining the major language skill components of writing, speaking, and reading good literature.

In building a whole language classroom, the teacher promotes a kind of teaching in which language is created and used by all pupils of all learning levels. The environment allows for the pupil to be immersed by all types of media, both print and electronic. Students write for a number of purposes in meaningful settings without the rigid structural guidelines imposed by the consideration of a single topic or issue. The content areas such as science and social studies provide a natural contextual environment. Daily observations are made by the alert teacher for the purpose of establishing appropriate individualized instruction for pupils who need help in specific language areas.

Recent education reports, such as one by the National Assessment of Education Progress (NAEP) entitled *Who Reads Best* recommends that reading educators move away from the overreliance on basal readers and accompanying workbooks and more toward a greater emphasis on comprehensive strategies, more independent reading for children, and more opportunities for the meaningful combination of reading and writing activities. Literacy experts are demanding this new thrust in reading instruction to help insure that the young adult entering the workplace of the 21st century can demonstrate skills in all of the language areas, because noted reading educators now contend that reading, writing, and speaking develop interrelatedly rather than a large grouping of minute skills.

Many state departments of education have engaged in massive and sweeping reforms in the area of reading instruction. California, for example, has instituted a new reform plan which calls for the formation of a systematic literature program with a meaning-centered approach based on intensive reading, writing, speaking, and listening. The ultimate goal of the California program, as well as those of other states, is to build student reading interest to a high level without diminishing basic levels in the significant reading skill areas of word attack, comprehension, and vocabulary.

Nearly all of the in-service elementary teachers in the United States have had preservice training in the use of standard basal reading materials with concomitant proficiency in teaching pupils from a scope and sequence approach involving hundreds of skill strands. There is a clamor among educators across the country for a well-developed, easy-to-read volume that emphasizes the whole language-literature approach to reading. *This textbook addresses this need.* The well-developed procedures described in this volume are the products of the author's 43 years experience as an elementary teacher, principal, and supervisor as well as a reading clinic director and coordinator of a graduate reading program at a major midwestern university.

Chapters I and II describe the reading process and a description of some of the major approaches to reading instruction. Chapter III emphasizes the whole language approach and describes how these strategies can benefit a reading curriculum. Chapters IV, V, and VI explain important methods for building word attack, comprehension, and content reading skills. The focus of Chapter VII deals with a literature-based curriculum and cooperative learning. Evaluating the reading program is explained in Chapter VIII. Three important appendices conclude the volume.

# ACKNOWLEDGMENTS

The author wishes to acknowledge his indebtedness to numerous persons who have been of tremendous assistance in the preparation of this volume. Appreciation is extended to Mrs. Jean Rutledge for her considerable help in locating materials and references for the various chapters. Mrs. Becky Schnabel acted as the official courier for the author and a "thank you" is accorded to her.

Sincere appreciation is extended to Mrs. Jan Wiebe, the manuscript typist, for her efficient and dedicated work on this, her fifth volume for the author. Her suggestions for certain changes in the various chapters helped in the total body of material.

Thanks is extended to Mr. Payne Thomas of Charles C Thomas, Publisher, for permission to utilize certain segments of material from two earlier volumes written by the author. Finally, I wish to thank my wife, Rita, for her patience and understanding during the long period of time consumed in the preparation of the manuscript.

# CONTENTS

# BUILDING ELEMENTARY READING SKILLS
# THROUGH WHOLE LANGUAGE AND LITERATURE

# CHAPTER I

# UNDERSTANDING THE READING PROCESS

In order to build an effective program of reading instruction for pupils of all ability levels, one must understand the essential and component parts of the reading process. While there is some divergence of opinion regarding the nature of the reading act, most authorities believe that learners must develop the skill of perceiving print and comprehending the meaning of the symbols based on their level of schemata. The construction of a basic body of reading competencies holds a high priority in the minds of both educators and the lay public and should receive appropriate attention at all levels of the school system. Grasping a sound understanding of the importance of reading skill development as a segment of the total curriculum is fundamental if elementary teachers are to teach reading competencies to the thousands of young people who are enrolled in the schools of this nation.

In order to provide appropriate background and insight for this vital area of the curriculum, the following topics are discussed in Chapter I. They are: definition of reading; the reading act; principles of effective reading instruction; and skills necessary in an effective elementary reading program. A summary and a body of appropriate references conclude the chapter.

## DEFINITION OF READING

During the past century, dozens of educators and psychologists have attempted to define *reading*. Nearly every text on reading proposes a definition of reading. The common elements in all of these definitions are that reading involves print, language, and comprehension.[1] There are some persons who place major emphasis on the pupil's ability to pronounce the words aloud in a fluent manner while others believe that the end product of any reading act must be comprehension that is based on the reader's background of understanding. Presently, a significant number of professionals believe that reading must be thought of as a part

3

of a whole language curriculum that places reading as a component part of a well-devised program of studies that relates reading, writing, speaking, and listening in an integrated nature. The emphasis is away from a skills-dominated curriculum to one that blends a body of competencies in a natural setting and views reading skill development as a process rather than an isolated subject.

There are certain aspects of the definition of reading that are somewhat common to all of the philosophies that have been espoused by various professionals. They are as follows:

1. **Reading is much more than the mere turning of letters into sounds.** Nor does reading involve processing each letter separately.[2]

2. **Reading provides an appropriate avenue for the sequential development and enlargement of affective as well as cognitive skills and attitudes.** While one of the major goals of reading is that of acquiring cognitive facts and concepts, one must also utilize the activity to develop positive self-concepts and realize that it is a suitable medium for enjoying the thoughts and ideas of authors who lived hundreds of years ago. Reading certain selections can affect the attitudes and perceptions of persons toward issues and forces of the greater society that may impact them both favorably and unfavorably.

3. **Reading is a multifaceted process that, like a chameleon, changes its nature from one developmental stage to the next.**[3] From birth to the beginning of formal reading instruction, the young learner normally develops appropriate readiness skills in the areas of motor development, auditory and visual competencies, spoken language proficiency, and listening abilities. Later, the pupil gains skill development in the areas of word analysis components (phonics, syllabication, structural analysis), general vocabulary, comprehension skill strands, and oral reading. Educators must understand that although various learners have similar patterns of reading skill growth, there is a great disparity in the time schedules when they arrive at certain guideposts in the skill sequence. Other factors affecting reading growth include pupil reading interest level; mental, social, and physical growth; and the environmental conditions under which the child is living.

4. **Reading is not a learning segment that emphasizes the acquisition of factual knowledge as an end in itself.** Teachers should welcome and encourage the active involvement of children in learning. Our teaching procedures should be a source of encouragement for all pupils to explore their world. Ours is an era in which the emancipation of the learner has

occurred, and more humane liberal and psychologically real conceptions about reading have emerged.[4]

5. **The acquisition of positive attitudes toward the process of reading should begin as early as the kindergarten level and should closely mirror the reading and writing experiences that pupils have encountered previous to entering school.** Pupils can develop a sufficient level of reading readiness if they are immersed in a variety of experiences such as the reading of big books, engaging in language experience activities, writing with invented spellings, and constructing word banks. Those who come to the kindergarten class ready or actually reading continue their growth as they learn large numbers of words and letter-sound associations through shared reading and writing experiences.[5]

6. **Because of the complex nature of reading skill development, it is extremely difficult to render a simple definition for the term.** As noted in the next section, the process of reading involves a variety of facets including sensory, perceptual, experiential, and cognitive areas. If children are to be proficient readers, it is necessary for them to have definitive competencies in all of these components. For example, while perception of symbols is important, learners must also have a sufficient level of schemata to interpret the symbols and make appropriate inferences relating to the true meaning of the print material.

7. **Many definitions of reading are value-laden, hypothetical statements of what reading ought to be, not neutral statements of what reading is in the strictly definitive sense.**[6] The meaning that is given to reading often reflects the point of emphasis of the individual giving the explanation or definition. Those who perceive reading to be mainly an act of word analysis places much importance on the phonic and perceptual skills of the learner. Others point out that reading is merely a significant part of a body of whole language that embodies reading, writing, speaking, and listening skills. Those who are advocates of the "top-down" approach to reading place heavy importance on the total schemata of the reader, whereas those who prefer the "bottom-up" approach perceive that major meaning comes from the printed passage itself instead of the total body of background knowledge that a learner may possess.

To the informed public, learning to be an effective reader of all types of printed materials is of the highest importance. There are a number of reasons for general society's concern about the proficiency of a given pupil's skill development in reading. *First,* the elementary pupil who exhibits a significant level of reading deficiency may be the object of ridicule on the part of his or her peers, family, and friends. **Second,** reading allows the young child to acquire basic concepts and data relating to the essential content core curriculum areas such as social studies, science, and mathematics. **Third,** children need to aspire to be well-informed agents of society and be aware of those aspects that will allow them to be good citizens and efficient professional workers.

During the middle grades, each pupil must develop independence in study habits in order to learn the basic concepts necessary for coping with reading tasks related to various content area subjects. An individualized reading program based on the premises of whole language instruction provides a firm foundation for allowing pupils to understand the importance of the reading process as a tool for gaining a body of new knowledge.

## THE READING ACT

One of the most interesting questions concerning reading is what takes place in the minds of readers as they actually read. The act requires numerous processes including sensory, perceptual, sequential, experiential, thinking, learning, association, and affective.[7] Understanding how these processes interact is important if the teacher is to comprehend fully how the young learner approaches the reading assignment. The following are some of the major aspects of the reading act.

I. **A major component of the reading act consists of the integration of all of the sensory avenues such as hearing and seeing.** For example, reading is, first of all, a visual act and it cannot ever be taught soundly if the functions of the eye are not understood. Proper coordination of the eyes, the true eye span possible, the obstacles to successful reading in faulty movement patterns, and various common visual defects must be understood by classroom teachers if they are to be successful.[8] The way the eyes function is important to the final level of success the learner may achieve. The eyes move across the page and make a number of stops called *fixations.* Those who find it necessary to look back at words for further reinforcement find that these *regressions* impede the spread of reading to a considerable extent. Some elementary and secondary students succumb to the advertisements of speed reading schools that "guarantee" the doubling of reading speed without any loss in comprehension. Some reading authorities are prone to doubt the claims since readers cannot read any faster than they can comprehend.

*Auditory discrimination* must be developed at a very proficient level since the precise determination of the likenesses and differences in sounds is vital to understanding the exact nature of the phoneme-grapheme relationship of various sounds. The development of writing and speaking skills is based on the correct auditory input from listening to parents, peers, and teachers. Obviously, the teacher should refer children to a hearing specialist such as an otologist if they exhibit such manifestations as turning the head to hear better, facial expressions suggesting a hearing problem, or requests to have oral directions repeated frequently.

**II. Word analysis or the decoding of words is thought to be the center or core of the act of reading by many reading specialists.** Many kindergarten children arrive the first day of school with the proficiency to say hundreds of words. Since they have not had formal instruction in such basic skill segments as phonetic and structural analysis principles, sight word vocabulary, and context clues they are prone to have major difficulties in identifying the printed word that stands for its spoken counterpart. In a well-designed program of reading instruction, the learners are exposed to a systematic skill program of word attack that will allow them to decode words with rapidity and meaning. The learning of various associations of a phonemic-graphemic nature and how to use context in conjunction with the association makes it possible to independently convert print symbols to speech symbols.[9]

**III. To maximize the full effects of the reading act, the learner should possess a broad schemata of understanding for the important words in any given sentence or paragraph.** Those authorities who subscribe to the "top-down" (reader-based) approach contend that learners must have a sufficient background of experience with the printed matter if basic meaning, hypotheses, and predictions are to be made. An analysis of the level and nature of the overall schemata of a given child can be determined through the administration of formal and informal tests as well as direct and planned oral questioning on the part of the teacher. Those pupils who demonstrate obvious limitations with regard to the understanding and meaning of words must be given instruction in vocabulary development that is based on the individualized needs of each child.

**IV. The end product of the reading act is the grasping of meaning and the message that the writer intended to convey to the reader.** There are some lay persons as well as professionals who place heavy emphasis on the decoding or pronouncing of words. Unfortunately, there are young as well as older readers who impress audiences with their ability to read orally but fail to display adequate competency in the area of communication with the author. Elementary reading teachers need to promote the four basic levels of comprehension that should be an inherent part of any well-established developmental reading skills program.

**Literal reading** involves such aspects as recall of details, specific facts, main ideas that are stated, a sequence of events, and distinct cause and effect relationships.

**Interpretive reading** requires the reader to select important main ideas, make significant comparisons in times, places, and characters; draw valid conclusions, and detect the mood and purpose of the writer.

**Critical reading** involves the ability of the learner to differentiate between fact and opinion, note propaganda techniques, and determine the overall accuracy of a given body of printed matter.

**Creative reading** demands that the reader develop an emotional response to a plot or theme, create appropriate reactions to the author's use of different types of language, make value judgments about the actions of characters, and use the text body for formulating new procedures or ideas. Detailed examples of sample questions to be used with each level can be found in Chapter V.

**V. After the reader has decoded the words and comprehended them, he or she integrates the new information obtained and makes it a part of the total schemata.** New vocabulary learned helps to enlarge the knowledge and experience base of the learner and helps to provide for a broad foundation of understanding as new words and phrases are encountered. To help the reader achieve this goal, the teacher may choose to engage in a meaningful culminating or general class activity that will serve to join all of megacognitive forces which may be present for any given reader.

**VI. Undertaking the reading act and enjoying success in the activity are positively correlated to the physical, mental, and experiential backgrounds of learners.** The most successful readers generally have an average to above average intelligence quotient, enjoy good physical health, and have had a wide background of experience that results in a broad schemata base of understanding. Young children who have decided reading deficiencies should be evaluated by both formal and informal tools to determine their level of abilities in these three important areas. Individualized lesson plans that integrate all phases of whole language (reading, writing, speaking, and listening) should be devised for each child based on his or her demonstrated strengths and limitations.

**VII. The reading act should be structured to help assure that the experience is enjoyable and profitable for the learner.** Unfortunately, too many children perceive reading to be a task-oriented activity whose major purpose is merely the memorization of a multiplicity of facts and figures to remember to be repeated on a class lesson sheet or test. They should understand that while the receptive phases of language (listening and reading) are valuable for receiving information, they can readily express their own feelings and understandings through a careful program of speaking and writing in a well-devised whole language teaching and learning environment.

In summary, one must understand in the *first* place that the reading act or process (if carefully undertaken) transforms the nonreader to one that acquires knowledge of various types from the printed page with speed and efficiency. For the beginning readers, they must develop linguistic and syntactical awareness and understand how reading works. They must recognize that the procedure involves left-to-right, top-to-bottom page orientation and that words have a predictable syntactical pattern in a sentence involving a subject, predicate, object, and modifiers.

*Second,* the young learner recognizes the word as a unit of speech and develops a knowledge of a basic stock of sight words such as recognizing his or her name, words relating to familiar objects, and words having multiple purposes.

*Third,* the pupil then typically grasps the skills relating to word analysis such as phonics and attempts to pronounce words independently. The phonological code of the language is developed along with an understanding of the sound-symbol relationships and the regular phonic units in words. Teachers help young readers apply skills by providing appropriate practice in meaningful settings.

*Fourth,* there is a gradual movement from word recognition skills to reading for understanding and the ideas that the author seeks to communicate to the reader. If the young learner is making natural skills acquisition growth, he or she becomes proficient with understanding more complex sentences involving numerous phrases. Competency is gained in dealing with the four major levels of comprehension in all of the significant content areas. Knowledge of both a cognitive and affective nature are developed to an optimum level.

*Fifth,* the final aspect of the reading act is consummated when the mature reader applies reading to many diverse and complex situations such as reading for recreational purposes, reading to gain a broad knowledge regarding a number of different topics, and reading for personal reasons.

These five steps denote a sequence of strategies that are developed during the natural progression of the refinement of the reading act. As noted earlier, these include the acquisition of linguistic structure, the meaning of words, the enlargement of vocabulary, understanding of various levels of comprehension questions, and reading of a broad nature that includes data and information for everyday living.

## PRINCIPLES OF EFFECTIVE READING INSTRUCTION

If an elementary reading program is to be effective, certain principles must be made an integral part of every phase of the instruction. The new emphasis on whole language and literature selections makes the total reading curriculum effective for all learning levels with pupils of various ability skills. To help insure that this condition is reached, the following guidelines should be a part of every reading program.

**I. Reading skills instruction should be only one part of an effective whole language curriculum.** Recent research data appear to indicate that teaching hundreds of reading subskills in isolation from meaningful writing, speaking, and listening activities results in less general language arts achievement than when they are integrated. Pupils can read a certain selection they have written and share their story with other learners while they listen with attention and purpose. Practice must be given at *all* age and learning levels to help insure that pupils learn the proper relationship between graphemes and phonemes and the correct manner for writing and saying the various syllabic segments that constitute a word or phrase. Integrating a regular program of language experience activities helps learners to see the correlation that is necessary between telling a story, writing it down, and reading it later.

Listening skills must be stressed. Pupils should be given a purpose for listening and taught to understand how listening, reading, writing, and speaking are related. Learning to speak and write new words is highly dependent on a child's ability to listen to word formations as they occur during television presentations and class discussions conducted by the teacher. Daily opportunities should be given for the total class to engage in meaningful, natural listening situations when specific purposes are given for learning precise data.

The chief author of *Becoming a Nation of Readers,* Richard Anderson, believes that the whole language movement is an attempt to restore the balance in reading programs. Many programs of the past have placed too much emphasis on small bits and pieces of knowledge and skills and gave too little attention to the integrated art of reading. He warns that although whole language has a desirable effect, one should be concerned that whole language extremists may demand too little structure without singling out a facet, one aspect or a bit of knowledge about language for special attention.[10]

**II. Teachers and administrators should provide a wide and diverse array of reading materials that will appeal to all age and interest levels of elementary pupils.** In addition to basal reading materials, newspapers, comic books, magazines, game instructions, bubble gum wrapper jokes, cookbooks, fortune cookie fortunes, puzzle books, novels, collections of short stories, and poetry should be offered. Each child will feel the intense joy of reading when he or she accidently stumbles on a favorite reading form and topic.[11] Attention should be given to the many supplementary reading materials suggested by basal reading publishers and leading reading authorities. Working in cooperation with the school media specialist the classroom teacher can present book reviews relating to new books that have been purchased recently. The Newberry and Caldecott Award winners should receive special attention.

At any one grade level the range of reading levels may be wide and diverse. To find these data some reading authorities use the formula two-thirds times the mean chronological age of the pupils enrolled in a given class. For example, at the fourth grade level when the M.C.A. may be 9, one might expect to find a six-grade reading level range. Theoretically, the teacher may find one or more pupils reading at the first-grade level and one or more reading at the seventh-grade level.

Because of these conditions, it is clear that no *one* particular reading level or content book can possibly serve the needs of all learners. Other books and articles may be in place in the school media center that would be appropriate for a particular assignment. Elementary pupils should be encouraged to find basic data and topic information from a variety of sources. A semi-individualized approach will permit each learner to succeed in reading at his or her *current* instructional reading level.

**III. Since there is a great diversity in the kinds of learning styles preferred by various pupils, the elementary reading teacher should utilize instructional approaches that require seeing, listening, and speaking activities.** Cognitive and affective reading skills are accrued more quickly and accurately when the teacher matches reading style elements with lesson plans. A commercial test entitled *Reading Style Inventory* (Learning Research Associates, P.O. Box 39, Roslyn Heights, New York 11577) measures numerous reading style elements such as environmental, emotional, sociological, and physical stimuli. An individual reading style profile can be produced for each learner indicating such aspects as perceptual strengths and preferences, preferred reading environment, emotional profile, sociological preferences, and physical preferences. Recommended strategies for teaching reading are included.

However, there are some reading educators such as Harris and Sipay,[12] who believe that until more evidence is available, it seems that for most children a balanced eclectic approach that uses visual, auditory, touch, and kinesthetic cues in combination, and develops word identification and comprehension simultaneously, seems safer and less likely to produce difficulties than any method that relies primarily on one sensory avenue or stresses one important side of reading while neglecting another.

**IV. For the elementary reading program to be effective, a well-devised plan for both the periodic and continuous evaluation of each pupil's reading strengths and limitations must be undertaken.** Included in the total plan should be commercial tests (including achievement and diagnostic measures) as well as teacher-constructed tests designed to measure specific class objectives related to the basic skill areas such as word attack, comprehension, and study skills. The use of a reading survey test such as the *Iowa Test of Basic Skills* may be extremely useful in charting pupil competencies in such areas as vocabulary and comprehension. There are several important individual diagnostic instruments such as the *Gates-McKillop-Horowitz Tests* that provide valuable data relating to skill development in oral reading, word attack, auditory blending and discrimination, spelling, and writing. Informal commercial instruments may be used effectively to discover the independent, instructional, and frustration reading levels of learners. Additional data may lead instructors to locate the specific reading problems of individual children. Names of such tests include *Burns/Roe Informal Reading Inventory* (Houghton Mifflin Company) and the *DeSanti Cloze Reading Inventory* (Allyn and Bacon, Inc.) Tests used on classroom computers that are related to adopted teaching materials such as basal readers or supplementary instructional series may lend valuable data relating to such components as word attack, vocabulary, and word meaning.

**V. The goal of making reading activities enjoyable and interesting**

**should be pursued with much vigor by every teacher.** At the outset, teachers should serve as role models by sharing books and stories they have read with their pupils. They can write the "poem of the day" or "today's joke" on the board. Other procedures may include the following:

1. Find new, interesting books that have been purchased recently for the room or school library. Read the introduction to selection and invite pupils to read the remainder of the story.

2. Play commercially prepared tapes or stories, poems, and other selections.

3. Conduct regularly scheduled conversations with pupils in order to learn about their reading interests. As a result of the visits, invitations may be extended to various pupils to share a story or poem with the total class.

4. Introduce learners to a new word each day. Discuss the unusual segments of the word, its meaning, and origin. Use the word in a sentence along with other sentences to build a short story.

5. To motivate pupils to read widely, the use of both intrinsic and extrinsic procedures should be employed. Some teachers extend "Good Reader" awards to all learners who read a certain number of books. Other school authorities are involved in *Pizza Hut's National Reading Incentive Program.* According to the plan, each child reads four books that contain at least 30 pages of words. At the conclusion of the reading of each volume, the reader gives an oral book report to a parent or guardian who in turn completes a form attesting that the books have been read. Pins and certificates for complimentary pizzas are awarded by Pizza Hut on a monthly basis to each child who completes the required reading.

6. Karlin and Karlin[13] believe that book displays also create interest in reading. They may consist of bulletin boards on which colorful pictures, comments, and questions attract attention. Dust jackets from books or a special theme or a noted author may be used. The purpose of the bulletin board is to keep class members informed about books they may want to read and to excite their interest in them.

7. There should be much opportunity given to students to respond to stories, poems, and other selections read in class. The freedom to respond is extremely important in any society committed to developing a nation of literates. Each person needs to feel that personal reactions, good and bad, prosaic or profound, are essential in developing critical appreciation and thinking.[14]

The major goal of a total program of effective reading instruction is to try to insure that all learners gain a satisfactory level of competence in the various skill areas and achieve an understanding that reading is an enjoyable and satisfying activity that can lead to a significant increase in both the cognitive and affective skill components. Reading should never be thought of as a dull subject to be endured but rather a body of competencies to be developed in *every* class activity that occurs during the school day. Every instructor is a teacher of reading and should emphasize all of the major skill areas during the school day.

## SKILLS NECESSARY IN AN EFFECTIVE ELEMENTARY READING PROGRAM

Regardless of the methods and materials used in any modern, innovative elementary reading program, there are various skill segments that should be constructed. The additional emphasis of utilizing whole language and cooperative learning to an established reading curriculum can help produce readers who enjoy reading to the fullest sense and understand how this input language segment correlates with speaking, writing, and listening. During the elementary school years pupils should build a significant body of cognitive and affective reading skills that will result in their ability to read and understand various kinds of reading material and view the art of reading as pleasurable and enjoyable.

**With respect to selected cognitive skills, pupils should be able to:**

1. Unlock words through the use of several different techniques such as phonetic analysis, structural analysis, context clues, and the use of the dictionary.

2. Understand and develop an ever increasing level of vocabulary in all of the major content study areas.

3. Read various types of printed material and answer questions relating to the literal, interpretive, critical, and creative levels of comprehension.

4. Utilize classroom and media references correctly when seeking certain pieces of informational data from specialized sources such as dictionaries, world almanacs, encyclopedias, and atlases.

5. Read orally with meaning and expression with a minimum of errors such as substitutions, omissions, repetitions, and hesitations.

6. Understand the place and importance of content textbook segments such as the preface, table of contents, glossary, and index.

7. Utilize the SQ3R reading-study formula (survey, question, read,

recite, review) in all content reading areas where it would facilitate the study and recollection of certain kinds and types of knowledge.

8. Use context clues to help clarify meanings of words and phrases within a larger body of material.

9. Know how to adjust reading rate of reading in light of the nature of the material being read and the stated purposes of the reader.

10. Achieve a sufficient level of readiness in the motor, auditory, visual, and vocabulary skills areas to help insure success in beginning reading experiences.

The previous list is merely a representative sampling of cognitive skills. The complete body of competencies that should be pursued may be determined by studying carefully the scope and sequence of an adopted reading series and the precise instructional needs of pupils both singularly and collectively. A whole language program that is supplemented by literature and a cooperative learning segment can be most helpful to all elementary teachers who want to be sure that their pupils have gained sufficient knowledge in the cognitive skill area.

**Major affective competencies should also be promoted in any viable elementary program.** Teachers should help pupils develop:

1. A broad interest in reading books, magazines, and stories in many different subject areas.

2. An understanding of the feelings and attitudes of writers, past and present.

3. The attitude that leisure time reading is an important expenditure of time when it results in reading for pure pleasure, fun, and excitement.

4. A feeling that a higher level of reading skill competency is directly related to one's ability to accumulate an ever-increasing body of overall knowledge of various types.

5. An appreciation for the beauty of thoughts and words as expressed in poems, stories, and different selections.

The previous cognitive and affective skills will by necessity have a different level of significance for learners at the primary, intermediate, and upper-grade divisions. For example, reading readiness is more important and urgent for primary learners while the advanced cognitive skills of critical reading, and study skills may be stressed more for older learners. A program of evaluation and measurement should be constructed using formal and informal instruments and strategies to measure the degree of proficiency obtained by the learners with regard to the adopted competencies. School staff members should constantly study the items to determine if they are relevant for the current pupils being served.

## SUMMARY

Reading is an important avenue through which most persons secure the ideas, thoughts, and revelations of persons who may have lived hundreds of years ago. There are many definitions for the terms that have been promoted by educational specialists.

The reading act is complex and includes such aspects as sensory avenues, background of experience, and learner attitude. The end product of the act is the recognition of the reader of the message or communication that the writer wishes to deliver.

The principles of any effective elementary program are described in this chapter and should be considered carefully by all teachers and administrators. These standards will help to insure a maximum level of success in building reading skills and attitudes.

Cognitive as well as affective skills should be promoted in any elementary reading program. The final list of goals established should be based on each learner's needs and learning level.

## REFERENCES

1. Finn, Patrick J. *Helping Children Learn to Read.* New York, Random House, 1985, p. 2.
2. Weaver, Constance, "What Is Reading . . . And How Can Our Definition Make A Difference?" *Reading Horizons: Selected Readings* (Second Edition) Kalamazoo, Western Michigan University, 1983, p. 33.
3. Spache, George D. and Evelyn B. Spache. *Reading In The Elementary School* (Fifth Edition). Boston, Allyn and Bacon, 1986, p. 4.
4. Harker, John, "The Reading Connection: Facts, Skills and Literacy—What is Reading For?" *Canadian Journal of English Language Arts*, Vol. 11, No. 2 (1988), p. 51.
5. Cunningham, Patricia M., "How Should Reading Be Taught in Kindergarten," *Educational Leadership*, Vol. 45, No. 1 (September, 1987), p. 83.
6. Harris, Theodore L. and Richard E. Hodges (Co-Editors). *A Dictionary of Reading and Related Terms.* Newark, International Reading Association, 1981, p. 264.
7. Burns, Paul C., Betty D. Roe, and Elinor P. Ross. *Teaching Reading in Today's Elementary Schools.* (Fourth Edition). Boston, Houghton Mifflin, 1988, p. 3.
8. Spache and Spache, p. 7.

9. Hafner, Lawrence E. and Hayden B. Jolly. *Teaching Children To Read* (Second Edition). New York, Macmillan, 1982, p. 5.

10. Goddard, Connie Heaton, "Putting Reading Research Into Practice," *Instructor*, Vol. 118, No. 3 (October, 1988), p. 9.

11. Andersen, Dennis R. and Sandra McCandless Simons, "The Seven Secrets of Success," *Instructor*, Vol. 118, No. 3, (October, 1988), p. 18.

12. Harris, Albert J. and Edward R. Sipay. *How To Increase Reading Ability* (Seventh Edition). New York, Longman, 1980, pp. 70–71.

13. Karlin, Robert and Andrea R. Karlin. *Teaching Elementary Reading Principles and Strategies* (Fourth Edition). New York, Harcourt Brace Jovanovich, 1987, p. 397.

14. Weiss, M. Jerry, "Writers and Readers: The Literary Connection," *The Reading Teacher*, Vol. 39, No. 8 (April, 1986), p. 759.

Chapter II

# UTILIZING EFFECTIVE APPROACHES
# TO READING INSTRUCTION

Educators at the present time are finding increasing pressure put on them by the general public to produce more able readers at all school divisions particularly at the elementary level. A spate of national reports seek to portray a steadily declining rate of achievement test growth in reading. A disenchantment on the part of some parents has caused many of them to establish home schools, send their pupils to private institutions, and enroll them in prestigious reading clinics. Many believe that some reading programs are ineffective and demand an immediate movement to a "back to basics" format.

These public pressures cause educators to study anew a basic question: "What is the most effective approach to use for reading instruction?" To help answer this question, this chapter is designed to help readers explore seven major topics: finding the best approach, basal reading instruction, language-experience approach, individualized reading, role and use of computer-assisted instruction, Chapter I reading programs, and alternatives to traditional reading programs.

A summary and body of references conclude the chapter. Chapter III is devoted exclusively to whole language while Chapter VII explores the values of promoting reading interest through a literature-based curriculum and cooperative learning.

## FINDING THE BEST APPROACH

As noted in the sections to follow, there are a number of major approaches that can be used to teach reading. *Even though each approach has significant advantages, the key element in any reading instructional program is the competency of the teacher. Books and other materials don't teach, teachers do.* The mere changing of one formal program to another does not guarantee immediate success for the affected students unless there has been a corresponding upgrading of reading skills instruction ability on the part of the teachers.

*Before* any approach is established, the following four questions must be addressed by the school staff:

1. **What skills and competencies do we want our students to develop?**
2. **What type of evaluation program will we establish to determine the present reading abilities of our pupils?**
3. **What kind of approach or techniques will we employ to help each learner improve reading deficiencies?**
4. **How will we determine if our teaching strategies are successful?**

Robinson and Hulett[1] believe that schools have tended to rely very heavily on standardized reading test results as a single measure of their effectiveness in reading instruction. They think that self-evaluation and questionnaires may give a much more accurate picture of what is taking place, especially if an atmosphere is developed for faculty to respond with candor and openness. After the program of evaluation takes place, teachers must be motivated to change in a nonthreatening atmosphere.

Before adopting or adapting any particular reading approach, one should dispel certain *myths* about the teaching of reading. The following is a list of beliefs held by many individuals. **First, some believe that every child will benefit from a good phonics program.** Marie Carbo[2] insists that phonics is a method, not a goal. Phonics is beneficial only if it helps a student to read fluently, with good comprehension, and if it's an enjoyable learning experience. Some pupils are not strongly auditory and analytic and have great difficulty discriminating among sounds and find phonics to be difficult and boring.

**Second, there are persons who are convinced that there is a rather precise, narrowly defined body of reading skills that should be mastered by all pupils.** On the contrary, all learners are at a different level of achievement and possess vast diversity in learning styles and preferred learning modalities. To impose a single scope and sequence of skills on all learners is both impractical and indefensible.

**Third, to build a strong base for reading skills development, pupils should be given a substantial amount of practice using workbook and duplicated worksheets.** This myth does not take into account the fact that many pupils are highly gifted with regard to reading achievement and the requirement of completing certain practice sheets over skills they already know is a tragic waste of instructional time. These pupils should be challenged to read in a wide variety of materials that will challenge and excite them. In every case, their instructional reading levels should be determined and appropriate teaching procedures instituted that correlate with each student's needs.

## Criteria for Evaluating the Worth of a Reading Approach

Finding the best approach to employ requires the use of several standards such as the following:

1. The approach is flexible and can accommodate the instructional needs of all students.
2. The general plan is functional and relatively easy to employ by teachers of all ability and experience levels.
3. There are definitive goals and objectives that are stated and can be developed.
4. The cost of the plan is reasonable and the teaching materials are durable.
5. The procedures encourage extended reading activities on the part of all students at all learning levels.
6. There are cognitive and affective skills components that accompany the plan.
7. It is possible for pupils to enter and leave the program with a minimum of difficulty for both teachers and learners.
8. There are definitive procedures in evidence for the continuous and periodic evaluation of each student's progress in reading achievement.
9. Provisions should be made for providing adequate time on task for each learner.
10. There is a clear relationship between the basic objectives of the reading program and the reading skills and competencies demanded by society in general.

The best approach selected for use for reading instruction should receive positive marks on all of the previous criteria and be well received by all persons involved in the educational process including parents, teachers, and students.

## BASAL READING INSTRUCTION

The oldest and most common approach for the teaching of reading is the basal reading system which was first originated about 1800. The *McGuffey Eclectic Reading Series* was first published about 1845 and continued without interruption until approximately 1920. The series consisted of a basic primer and six additional level readers and contained selections designed to teach basic human morals and standards for living. Current basal programs originated in the late 1920s with such series as the Elson-Gray readers published by Scott, Foresman and Company. At the present time there are approximately fifteen major publishers of basal readers. The vast majority of schools use a basal reading series as the core of reading instruction with additional teaching components such as language experience, programmed materials, whole-language, and literature-based items. The final product is an eclectic approach that combines the most satisfactory features of several methods.

Most of the basal series contain several significant components. The *level readers* constitute the core of the basal program and are usually arranged in a sequence of increasing difficulty from the reading readiness to the upper grade levels. Most companies have 13–16 readers; however, one major publisher has over 40 levels. Each of the readers contains stories that represent all cultural levels and avoid sex, race, and occupation stereotyping. The stories have been chosen carefully and are based on field-testing with students. The selections are collected from Caldecott and Newberry Award winners.

The *teacher's edition* for each level reader contains a multitude of teaching suggestions relative to a number of aspects including introduction of vocabulary, decoding of words, comprehension strategies, and enrichment reading activities. The materials have been researched to help insure their usability with all types of instructors with varying levels of teaching experience and background.

*Mid-level and level tests* accompany the series and are designed to help the teacher evaluate the degree of reading achievement obtained by each learner in order to determine the placement of pupils in the total program.

*Computer software* materials are available for computer assisted instruction (CAI) and computer managed instruction (CMI). The CAI lessons are designed to provide developmental and tutorial lessons while the CMI component allows the teacher to construct record-keeping printouts and evaluate student achievement through the use of specially constructed tests for diagnosis and coordinating prescriptions for individualized assignments.

*Miscellaneous components* involve such aspects as study books, booster activities, reading progress cards, pupil profile cards, wall charts, parent-home activity sheets and newspapers, and card sets.

Publishers invest millions of dollars and years of preparation time in their development; however Clary and Smith[3] believe there is no uniform method of selecting basals and little information is available on methods being used. They believe there are groups representing several points of view that need to be considered: state departments of education in the 23 adoption states, district selection committees, local reading specialists, reading educators, parents, students, and local boards of education.

**Basal reader series possess a number of advantages for educators and pupils.** They are well structured, present reading skills sequentially, and help schools to present a well coordinated reading curriculum for all of the learners. Additionally, the plan can be used with a great amount of success with teachers of varying levels of teaching experience.

Recently, publishers have made a concerted effort to include characters in their selections that represent various minority groups, nontraditional occupations, and handicapping conditions. The supplementary materials mentioned earlier are of significant help to all teachers in meeting the needs of children at various learning levels.

**Basal materials may possess certain limitations that are not inherent in the approach but rather in the way they are utilized by certain teachers.** Miller[4] believes that overdependence on the basal teachers' manuals may stifle teacher creativity if the manuals are used as a "Bible" instead of as a guide. Although the reading specialists who formulate basal reader series never plan on having their materials used in this limited way, in practice this sometimes happens. Other authorities[5] are of the opinion that some basal readers limit children's reading. Many basal readers, particularly those used for beginning reading, have been criticized for containing story material written in a style that is not typical of normal speech. Recently, most authors have made a concentrated effort to try to make the language more natural and correlated with current syntactical and semantic patterns.

In addition to the previous criticisms, some believe that a few teachers undertake practices that are inherent by-products of the steady, unrelenting use of basal materials. These include the rigid compliance of forming *three* reading groups, little or no provisions for individual differences, and the moving of all pupils at the same pace through the materials regardless of their current reading ability.

## LANGUAGE-EXPERIENCE APPROACH

The language-experience approach (LEA) is a holistic method for teaching reading that encompasses all four facets of communication — listening, speaking, reading, and writing. As the term suggests, the LEA uses the language and experience base of the learner to help him or her develop appropriate reading skills. The major goal of using this approach is to simplify and help the young learner understand that written words are simply spoken words that are put into print. The most telling advantage of LEA is that it uses the pupil's own language and background of experience as the foundation for constructing stories that can be used as the focus material for learning to read.

The method itself has a long and interesting history. Several teachers in experimental schools started using the procedures around 1890. The importance of the method was highlighted in *The Twenty-Fourth Yearbook of the National Society for the Study of Education* which was published in 1925. The writers of the reading section advocated the use of the language experience approach as a means of acquainting young readers with the important segments of successful reading. One of the foremost authorities in the development of language experience lessons in recent years has been Roach Van Allen. In one of his earliest publications he promoted the idea that there are three primary goals that should be pursued when using LEA to achieve a balanced reading program.[6] They include building an adequate sight vocabulary and overall proficiency in all of the other word attack skills; integrating reading with speaking, writing, and listening; and establishing a lifelong love of reading.

**There are several concepts and guidelines that should accompany the teacher's plan for the construction of the experience charts with small groups of pupils.** They include the following:

1. The stories that are written by the teacher on the chart paper should be based on some experience that the children and the teacher have had, are having, or will undertake in the future.
2. The material used on the charts should never be abstract but rather

a part of the pupils' total experience and something that they know about or have had a chance to observe on a first-hand basis.

3. It is incumbent that the teacher understand the basic ways in which vocabulary and language development unfolds in the normal development of young learners. This knowledge should be incorporated in the actual recording of the story on the sheet.

4. The construction of the various stories should be undertaken with the view that they will be reviewed and integrated properly with stories that are composed at a later date.

5. A word bank should be established whereby new vocabulary words are recorded on strips of cardboard and reviewed at regular intervals to help insure retention.

**If the language experience program is properly integrated with all other parts of a total whole language curriculum, there are a number of advantages that may be realized.** (The degree of importance that may be attached to each item may depend on variables such as the number of pupils enrolled in a given class, the teaching philosophy of the instructor, and the schemata or general background of experience that each child may possess.)

1. **The approach involves all four of the communication aspects— speaking, reading, listening, and writing.** The pupils *discuss* their experiences aloud, *read* the comments that the teacher has written, *listen* to the pronunciation of key words spoken by the teacher, and *write* word bank words on journal paper.

2. **The self-concepts of the students are enhanced because children select and create material that they value and reading thus becomes much more than an impersonal encounter with print.** Readers see themselves as being a vital foundation of the reading process.[7]

3. **The natural language of the pupils is utilized and tends to make the story selections more interesting and useful.** In all too many cases, many learners read only those commercial selections that have very controlled vocabularies and are based on mythical or make-believe experiences of imagined characters. The direct, local nature of the language experience stories creates a high level of excitement for the learners involved.

4. **The language experience approach can be of significant help in helping limited English speakers of all ages dictate text with expanded vocabulary and standard syntax according to a study conducted by**

**Moustafa and Penrose.**[8] The subjects were sheltered English, combination classes of 4th, 5th, and 6th graders in the early stages of English acquisition. Most of them spoke Spanish or Cambodian. The researchers instructed them in English language arts through comprehensible input plus LEA. At the end of the experiment period, 55 of the 58 students demonstrated a high comprehension retention by being able to go back and read again with ease stories that they had not studied for several months. They also demonstrated an ability to transfer what they had learned by reading with ease other groups' dictated stories.

In summary, language experience activities can be utilized as important adjuncts to a total whole language program that features cooperative learning and literature-based components.

## INDIVIDUALIZED READING

Some instructors use an individualized approach for the teaching of reading as a major method whereas others utilize the attributes of the approach as part of an overall eclectic curriculum. The approach is not new since it had its origins in rural one-teacher schools that have existed in this country since about 1800. The pupils in those schools ranged from grades 1 through 8 and ages 6 through 14 with individual and small group "recitations" for each learner. Most recently, Willard D. Olson published his plan for individualized reading in 1956 and involved three basic elements that were identified as *seeking, self-selection,* and *pacing.*[9] His viewpoint was that most children have established values and preferences for reading and seek and select those types of reading materials that will correlate with these traits. Pacing will be realized when he or she develops the desire to read increasingly more difficult books in various interest areas.

Those teachers who utilize individualized modes allow children to select a book or magazine selection that may be available in the classroom or school media center. He or she schedules two or more individual reading conferences each week with each learner at which time the teacher examines such components as the following:

1. The name of the material being read and the reasons offered for selecting that material.

2. The answers to specific literal, interpretive, critical, and creative questions that are asked.
3. The meaning of various words and phrases mentioned in the reading.
4. The future goals of the learner regarding the next book to be read.
5. Specific questions regarding a trade book just read by a learner may be asked. The following are sample questions.

    a. **What kind of story is this and what does it remind you of?**
    b. **What lesson, if any, did you remember from reading the book?**
    c. **Do you think this story could have actually taken place?**
    d. **Would you recommend this book to be read by your friends? Why or why not?**
    e. **What part of the story was your favorite?**
    f. **Why did you pick this book to read?**
    g. **Would you like to be anyone that was mentioned in the book?**
    h. **Would you like to live in the place where this story took place?**
    i. **Do you plan to read more books written by this author?**

There are a number of advantages that can be attributed to individualized reading procedures. *First,* learners are reading those selections that have a high level of interest and purpose for them as opposed to the "next" story in a basal reader that may not be of interest to them. *Second,* the conferences allow the teacher to concentrate on the exact reading skill strengths and attitudes of individual pupils. *Third,* there is less competitive stress among students since there is no direct comparison made with the reading skills growth of any other child in the room. *Fourth,* as noted earlier, the precepts of an individualized program can be used as the format for a general reading curriculum or as a part of a well-devised eclectic curriculum. It appears to have much potential as a significant part of a whole language program.

## ROLE AND USE OF COMPUTER-ASSISTED INSTRUCTION

Many educators began making use of computers to teach reading skills as early as the late 1950s and early 1960s. Universities such as Dartmouth and Stanford were the early educational leaders in developing basic drill and practice materials that were used extensively in many large school systems such as Chicago.

One of the earliest computer programs for reading instruction using a mainframe computer was the PLATO system developed by Donald Bitzer and his associates at the University of Illinois in the early 1970s. Since there was a single data source and pupils, in some cases, had to be moved to terminals away from the school building, the program was not advantageous for certain pupil groups. Because of the costs of hardware and the concurrent expenses of developing courseware, there was a decrease in the interest levels of many educators for incorporating computer assisted instruction in the mid 1970s. Additionally, some persons thought that computers had the potential for producing diminished levels of imagination on the part of learners. Robert J. Sardella, Director of Studies at the Dallas Institute of Humanities and Culture, charged in 1984 that "computer-dominated schools will create a generation of psychopaths because 'the psychopath does everything effortlessly, freely, without any sense of inhibition, restraint, or suppression.'"[10]

One of the leading advocates of computer assisted instruction is Dr. George E. Mason, Professor of Reading Education at the University of Georgia. He believes computers have a variety of uses such as a tool for diagnostic testing and as a provider of appropriate repetition for those learners who need additional skill practice. Leo D. and Olga P. Geoffrion note that there are numerous advantages to computer use with reading instruction.[11] They include (a) the novelty aspect that motivates the pupil to engage in numerous reading activities; (b) flexible features such as programming adjustments to allow for the various interests and needs of the user; and (c) the presentation of lessons that are fascinating and include multicolored animated illustrations, diagrams, charts, and tables at a fraction of the cost of a textbook.

## Types of Computer Software

At present, there are several kinds of computer software that are available for use by elementary teachers. The names of some of the various software pieces that are a part of each type can be found in the computer materials catalogues published by many companies.

### I. *Drill and Practice*

This type of software was one of the first kinds to be computerized. The exercises are presented in a homework activity format and are designed in such a manner to allow for the immediate correction of a student's answer to a particular question. Many companies produce the software packages that present the lessons at increasing levels of difficulty. Many publishers of basal reading materials produce these lessons to correlate with the selections that are presented in the different level readers.

## II. *Word-Processor Programs*

Many schools promote the use of the microcomputer as a word processing tool that eliminates the tedious tasks of writing, editing, and correcting since the cursor can be moved to change, rearrange, or eliminate individual words in a preliminary copy of an essay or article that is being composed. Some pieces of equipment have the capacity to correct misspelled words. Many teachers use such programs as the *Bank Street Writer* and the *Kidwriter* to allow learners to construct fictional stories, record language experience stories composed by the class, and formulate various types of lessons and short selections that are a natural outgrowth of a unit topic.

## III. *Tutorial Lessons*

Software designed for tutorial lessons may introduce new facts or concepts or they might be reviews of previous exercises that have been presented. A unique aspect of the software is branching modes that shifts the attention of the learner to review-type exercises if a certain level of competency is not attained in the regular program sequence. The *Tutorial Comprehension-Sequence* (Random House) is one such program that introduces the student to the meaning and use of various words and provides direct instruction and practice for identifying a sequence of events in a selection.

## IV. *Computer-Managed Programs*

These types of programs can help teachers keep track of student performance and guide learning activities. For example, some systems provide tests on specific objectives that are computer scored. The computer then matches the student's deficiencies to available instructional materials, suggests instructional sequences for the teacher to use or assigns material directly to the student.[12] Many publishers of basal reading and similar instructional programs offer software packages for evaluation of student achievement progress. They also have the capacity for recording grades from one learning level to another. The computer printer types the desired data to allow the instructor to tear off the sheet.

The sheet can then be placed in the pupil's folder for use during parent-teacher conferences.

### V. *Thinking and Problem-Solving Programs*

Some software has been developed to test students' ability to analyze higher-level thinking activities and problem situations. Various situational settings are devised in the form of a challenge game to allow students to solve various problems. For example, one piece of software provides a situation whereby the learner assumes the role of a basketball coach who was required to recruit outstanding players who would help assure a favorable won-loss record.

Though there are a large number of commercial software packages available for both computer-assisted and computer-managed instruction, the selection of items to purchase should be made with considerable discretion.

The following are several questions that should be utilized when evaluating a given program for possible use in an elementary classroom.

1. **What is the instructional range of the material and is the reading difficulty level appropriate for the learners I am teaching?**
2. **What is the basic nature of the software—drill and practice, simulation, tutorial, or thinking and problem solving?**
3. **Is the material user-friendly including simple directions and responses, minimum assistance from the teacher, and easy to understand?**
4. **Are the displays on the screen clear and easy to read with suitable margins and overall spacing?**
5. **Are the software pieces durable and useful over a reasonable period of time?**
6. **Is the program format constructed to promote maximum motivation and interest?**
7. **Are the exercises used for drill and practice and tutorial purposes correlated with the latest knowledge relating to the research regarding methods and materials?**

If the use of computers is to be an integral part of the overall reading instructional program, each teacher needs to have a common set of goals and objectives that are followed. The Omaha, Nebraska Public Schools developed the following plan of operation for all Chapter I teachers who make extensive use of computers in their classroom.[13]

*Goals and Objectives*

I. Know the reading software.

1. Be able to run 10–15 reading programs. Keep notes on these.
2. Identify idiosyncracies in various programs.
3. Know what to tell students about the program.

II. Know how to assign students to a specific program.
1. Know the student's learning needs.
2. Know the skills in each program.
3. Match student with appropriate program.

III. Have an entry and record-keeping process.
1. List the program and students to use the program. Assign students as part of reading prescription to use the program.
2. Have a form for the student to record:

> Program
> Practices
> Score

3. Keep a master record for teacher to mark.
4. Know how to organize a classroom for using the computer.

IV. Operating the computer.
1. Know how to operate the computer.
2. Know the terms used to describe specific operations.
3. Know how to run programs.
4. Know how to show students how to operate computer and run programs.

The amount of computer instruction will no doubt increase tremendously in the years ahead. New programs are being developed by numerous manufacturers for sale to both school officials and parents. There appears to be considerable evidence to suggest that computers have much potential as a learning aid for pupils at all learning levels. Pupils with little creative potential can utilize tutorial and skill-practice programs by merely pushing keys and following the simple directions that appear on the computer screen. Those who are more creative find the thinking and problem-solving segments to be challenging. To achieve maximum growth in reading achievement requires the combined efforts of the learners, their parents, and teachers. The mere placement of a child in front of a computer terminal for a full day schedule of lessons will not insure total success in reading.

The computer can serve as an important adjunct to any teacher who is pursuing different educational objectives with various learners. All instructors need to be knowledgeable about the latest trends and products attention needs to be given especially to the nature and kinds of software purchased. The quality of such materials has a wide latitude from outstanding to grossly inferior software being offered to the general public.

## CHAPTER I READING PROGRAMS

Chapter I, formerly called Title I, was part of the Elementary and Secondary Education Act which was passed by Congress in 1965. A cumulative total of almost forty-seven billion dollars has been spent since that time for all phases of the ESEA with a significant percentage allocated for Title I programs, especially those that emphasize reading.

The typical "Chapter I" school usually consists of one or more remedial reading and mathematics teachers who have special rooms that are stocked with a variety of printed materials, reading machines, and one or more computers. These types of classes are generally called "pull-out" programs that serve students who scored below the 50th percentile in reading comprehension on the most recent standardized achievement test that has been administered during the past 18 months. If they are attending a special education class such as one for the learning disabled, they may not be eligible for Chapter I classes.

During a designated class period, those pupils who are designated "Chapter I" report to the remedial reading teacher. (Due to certain high court decisions regarding the denial of public school teachers to teach in private school buildings, some districts have purchased mobile teaching vans that are driven to private school locations. Pupils in the private schools who are qualified for Chapter I services exit the school building and report to the public school mobile van for their lessons.)

The well-developed Chapter I reading program has a number of identifiable characteristics.

1. **The Chapter I teacher has constructed specific learning objectives for each learner which are correlated with the goals of the classroom teacher.**
2. **The lesson plans are individualized as much as possible to help insure maximum reading achievement growth for each child.**
3. **There are many teaching materials available that are useful and practical for students with numerous preferred learning modalities.**
4. **Lesson strategies are based on the results obtained from a broad-**

based program of reading evaluation that is constructed with both commercial and informal testing strategies. Computer-assisted instruction is used for those learners who can profit from these techniques.

5. Use various promotional activities to give status to those who attend the classes. In too many instances, pupils feel they are "stupid" and thus feel stigmatized in the total program. They should be made to understand that going to a Chapter I reading class is an *opportunity,* not a punishment.

With regard to Chapter I funding, the money goes to more than 90 percent of the nations 16,000 school districts and to 70 percent of the nation's elementary schools. This extra money—about $500 per eligible child—goes to pay for a variety of items such as professional salaries and materials for the classes.[14] *A basic question that has been asked in recent years relates to the amount and kind of reading achievement that has resulted from the vast array of Chapter I programs.* Slavin[15] notes that the problem with Chapter I is not the *amount* of funds it provides and not even how concentrated these funds are, but the *programs* that these funds buy. He contends that the programs are simply not designed for the job they are supposed to do. Traditional, diagnostic-prescriptive, pull-out programs make little lasting difference in student achievement. More effective programs are continuous progress models, cooperative learning programs, intensive supplementary programs, and computer-assisted instruction. As a final suggestion, Slavin believes for $500 per student, Chapter I in itself may not be able to "break the cycle of poverty." For five dollars per student we can certainly break the cycle of poor programs for students at risk.

Chapter I reading programs are an important adjunct to an otherwise effective reading curriculum but they must be more carefully tailored to meet the needs of the students they serve. Descriptions for many proven, effective reading programs can be found in the latest edition of *Educational Programs That Work* compiled by the U.S. Office of Education Joint Dissemination Study Group and published by Sopris West Incorporated, 1120 Delaware Avenue, Longmont, Colorado 80501.

## ALTERNATIVES TO TRADITIONAL READING PROGRAMS

Many educators are exploring alternative strategies for teaching reading skills besides a strictly basal materials approach. While the basal approach is suitable for most children, other learners require adaptations in the teaching-learning environment for achieving maximum results. Several of these approaches are described briefly in the section to follow.

## Writing to Read Program

The I.B.M. company has developed a reading program that involves a writing laboratory and various work stations. Most schools utilizing the program establish a separate classroom that contains a number of computers, several typewriters, a variety of tape-recorders, and the software and tapes that are necessary for the correct functioning of the equipment. Most teachers construct four or five stations in the room including *the typewriter station* where pupils can compose their compositions; *the listening station* where the tape-recorders are found; *the work journal station* where learners can write in a specially designed book while listening to the taped directions; the *games and activity station* where pupils can play structured word games and construct puzzles, and *the computer station* where different learner's can respond to directions from the software.

Though there is flexibility built into the program depending on student need and teacher competency, there are some general characteristics that are common to many of the program elements.

1. Phonics principles are taught through the use of key words that are commonly referred to as *cycle words.* The synthetic approach is used to allow the learner to hear the separate phonemes that constitute each word.
2. Pupils are encouraged to be creative and use invented spellings if necessary while they work at the writing station. A variety of subjects are introduced to discourage individual pupils from "copying" the topics and reading selections of their neighbors. Time should be given daily to all students to allow them an opportunity to create their own selections.
3. The typewriters are used generally by the pupils to compose their own selections; however, they may be used for self-constructed poems and riddles. The pursuit of the mastery of the typewriter instrument should allow for a significant amount of exploration of the numerous keys.
4. The games station may be used for a wide variety of purposes such

as word and letter games and activities employed for teaching phonic skills. Kinesthetic motor activities such as making words and letters out of clay and pipe-cleaner wires may be undertaken.

5. I.B.M. provides award-winning books and tapes for use with the tape-recorders. Students follow along visually in the books as they listen to the stories being read on the tapes.

There are a number of advantages that may be noted for the program. *First,* the prescribed program allows teachers of varying levels of ability to promote creative writing on a daily basis. *Second,* the activities tend to build independent work habits on the part of the pupils since it is necessary for them to move from station to station and record their individual rates of progress. *Third,* the level of communication is increased between the student and teacher. The creative writing selections reveal little known personal feelings such as family crises such as a death or a divorce. *Fourth,* the *Writing to Read Program* correlates well with any reputable basal program, including those with a whole language emphasis.

## Other Reading Programs

Eldredge and Butterfield[16] undertook an extensive one-year study of 26 classrooms using five experimental alternative reading strategies and compared them with 24 rooms using traditional basal materials approaches. Children using three alternative approaches produced better results on the *Gates-MacGinitie Reading Test* and a special phonics test than those in basal programs. The most successful programs included (1) *Basal program with heterogeneous grouping and 10–15 minutes of a special decoding program;* (2) *Individualized literature-based reading program;* and (3) *Literature program augmented with a 10–15 minute special decoding program.* The researchers note that if teachers and administrators want to try alternatives to traditional reading instruction without fear of losses in achievement, they have support from this study.

Before adopting or adapting any particular approach for the teaching of reading, educators should study carefully the various criteria that should be used for evaluating the worth of a reading approach as described at the beginning of this chapter. As noted, many aspects such as the available budget, school philosophy, teacher competency, and student goals should be carefully considered.

## SUMMARY

The decision regarding the best reading approach to use has been a lingering concern for educators for many years. Public outcrys for better reading programs make it necessary to select a reading approach that allows for maximum success on the part of both students and teachers.

Among the approaches that can be chosen are the basal materials method, language experience procedures, computer-assisted strategies, individualized reading methods, Chapter I reading programs, and a variety of alternative programs that are described in the last part of this chapter. Currently, many educators are choosing whole language and literature-based programs that involve cooperative learning components. (A description of this program is included in the next chapter.)

As noted, there are a number of criteria that should be applied before any approach is adopted or adapted for a given group of pupils. It is important to remember that while some approaches are more useful than others, the overall ability of the teacher is the most important single ingredient relating to the success of *any* reading program.

## REFERENCES

1. Robinson, Richard D. and Joycelin Hulett, "Reading Program Evaluation: A Plan For Effective Implementation," *Reading Horizons,* V.24, N.1 (Fall, 1983), pp. 40–41.
2. Carbo, Marie, "Ten Myths About Teaching Reading," *Teaching K-8,* V.17, N.6 (March, 1987), p. 77.
3. Clary, Linda Mixon and Susan Jeter Smith, "Selecting Basal Reading Series: The Need For A Validated Process," *The Reading Teacher,* V.39, N.5 (January, 1986), pp. 390–391.
4. Miller, Wilma H., *Teaching Elementary Reading Today.* New York, Holt, Rinehart and Winston, 1984, p. 104.
5. Robinson, Richard and Thomas L. Good. *Becoming An Effective Reading Teacher.* New York, Harper & Row, 1987, p. 76.
6. Van Allen, Roach. *Perspectives in Elementary Reading.* New York, Harcourt Brace Jovanovich, 1973, p. 162.
7. Robinson and Good, p. 79.
8. Moustafa, Margaret, "Comprehensible Input PLUS The Language Experience Approach: A Long-Term Perspective," *The Reading Teacher,* V.41, N.3 (December, 1987), pp. 276–286.
9. Olson, Willard D. *Psychological Foundations of The Curriculum* (Educational Studies and Documents, Number 26). New York, UNESCO, 1956, pp. 36–37.

10. Hechinger, F.M., "Teaching By Computer May Hurt Imagination," *The Omaha World-Herald* (July 18, 1984), p. 8.
11. Geoffrion, Leo D. and Olga P. Geoffrion. *Computers and Reading Instruction.* Reading, Massachusetts, Addison-Wesley, 1983.
12. Burns, Paul C., Betty D. Roe, and Elinor P. Ross. *Teaching Reading on Today's Elementary Schools* (Fourth Edition). Dallas, Houghton Mifflin, 1988, p. 335.
13. —— Using Computer Programs in Chapter I. Omaha, Omaha Public Schools Reading Services Center, 1984, p. 1.
14. Savage, David G., "Why Chapter I Hasn't Made Much Difference," *Phi Delta Kappan,* V.68, No. 8 (April, 1987), pp. 582–583.
15. Slavin, Robert E., "Making Chapter I Make A Difference," *Phi Delta Kappan,* V.69, N.2 (October, 1987), pp. 110–112.
16. Eldredge, J. Lloyd and Dennie Butterfield, "Alternatives To Traditional Reading Instruction," *The Reading Teacher,* V.40, No. 1 (October, 1986), pp. 32–37.

**Chapter III**

# TEACHING READING THROUGH WHOLE LANGUAGE STRATEGIES

One of the most important influences relating to current reading instruction is the infusion of an integrated language arts process called *whole language*. While whole language instruction has been an integral part of reading programs in Australia, New Zealand, and Canada for many years, the implementation of the procedures in American schools is a somewhat recent phenomenon.

There are many definitions and descriptions of whole language activity curricula. Because whole language is making a serious impact on the present and proposed elementary reading programs of this country, the purpose of this chapter is to address three significant topics relating to this topic. They are (1) principles of whole language instruction; (2) strategies for implementing a whole language curriculum; and (3) evaluating the effects of whole language instruction. A summary and a body of references conclude the chapter.

## PRINCIPLES OF WHOLE LANGUAGE INSTRUCTION

A perusal of the large volume of educational print and nonprint media reveals a wide divergence of opinion regarding the exact nature of the basic constructs of a reading curriculum that embodies the basic tenents of the whole language. Accordingly, proposing *the* definition for whole language is a very challenging task. There are some philosophical segments that appear to be noted by many educational authorities.

1. Whole language is not a precise approach but rather a body of beliefs that reading and general language skills and competencies are acquired through carefully integrated *use* and not by the direct emphasis of teaching dozens of finite skills relating to such areas as word attack, comprehension, and vocabulary.
2. Students in whole language classrooms are involved with many

39

kinds of print media and only very limited use is made of books and practice materials for the specific goal of teaching reading, writing, and listening. Kenneth Goodman[1] recommends that teachers put aside the carefully sequenced basal readers, spelling programs, and handwriting kits. Let the readiness materials, the workbooks, and the ditto masters gather dust on the shelves. Instead invite pupils to use language.

3. Content areas such as science and social studies provide unique opportunities for language growth since student learning is based on collaboration and close cooperation of the affected students.

4. Assessment of pupils is structured on constant observation and on actual competency growth that is based on the direct observed work of learners rather than a one-on-one comparison of scores on traditional achievement tests.

5. Large blocks of time are set aside for recreational reading—a lost luxury in the traditional classroom setting. Rather than spending time teaching isolated skills, teachers concentrate more effort on motivation.[2]

6. Pupils are grouped according to their learning needs when small skill segments are formed. Only those skills and competencies that are profoundly needed are emphasized by the instructor.

7. Whole language teachers believe there is something special about human learning and language and therefore encourage pupils to use the creative language that comes naturally to them. While high expectations are made of children's learning, instructors directly assist students to insure that expectations are accomplished.[3]

8. Pupils in whole language classrooms are encouraged to complete large amounts of creative writing and spell all words the best they can even if it means using "invented" spelling (e.g., *plak* for *plaque; crak* for *crack; mins* for *mince.*)

9. Judith Newman[4] warns that an overemphasis on accurate spelling, punctuation, and neat handwriting can actually produce a situation in which children come to see the conventions of writing as more important than the meaning they are trying to convey.

10. Children in whole language classes do not need to be told how to write, they need to be shown. Whole language teachers write along with their students. Teachers need to support and cheer students on, not wipe out their first efforts and early enthusiasm.[5]

11. Teachers who create whole language classrooms must involve

children in a variety of experiences that reflect many purposes of how language is served up outside the world of school. Keeping language "whole" requires classrooms that maintain the social, functional, and aesthetic aspects of language.[6]

12. Developing whole language classrooms demands a new mindset on the part of the teacher with the knowledge that it is not a new fad or *program* but a complete new *attitude* about integrating all of the language arts.

13. The real use of language must be established through the formulation of a philosophical base that views all of language components as a *natural* process and creates the feeling that pupils must always be thought of as consumers of language rather than subjects compelled to learn endless arrays of minute skills that have little, if any, everyday use for the average child.

14. Whole language *should not* be confused with the language experience or open education philosophies. Pupils can learn new vocabulary, syntax patterns, and styles from creative written language as opposed to the mere recording of language spoken by another person.

15. Many whole language teachers model language skills and allow for meaningful practice time for pupils to design and refine their own reading and writing abilities. Learners are thought of as social beings and not as individual robots who are obliged to complete a large set of sequentially developed skill books.

From a thoughtful study of the previous principles, one can make a number of careful observations. Most pupils, by and large, acquire sufficient levels of language training in their diverse environments to allow them to construct a substantial group of techniques and strategies that will allow them to communicate adequately with their fellow human beings. Vocabulary building begins at an early age and expands rapidly during the early years of life if a satisfactory school and home environment is in place that stimulates and challenges language learning.

Educators have come to realize that many young pupils can, and do, experiment with all kinds of spoken and written messages. They develop their own modes and styles of oral and written communication. Unfortunately, before the influence of whole language practices, teachers felt it necessary to stop and "correct" the oral language errors of pupils and thus developed an inherent fear among many learners about their ability to speak correctly. Numerous red check marks on written work created the impression that rules dictated production rather than simple creativity.

In many classrooms, children are no longer treated as partners in conversation since teachers generally decide what is going to be talked about and thus the pupils are less free to ask questions since it is all too obvious that the nature and emphasis of any given topic of conversation is the perogative of the teacher.[7] Pupils should be given much freedom to discuss openly many topics that are relevant and current for them. Teachers should encourage freedom of expression in the mode that seems most natural for the learner. Communication of ideas is the major goal rather than a strict evaluation of whether a particular pupil is following a set pattern of grammatical or syntactical structure.

Pupils should feel a sense of "ownership" about the topics they choose to write about. They need to experiment with words without the fear that a set of arbitrary rules will impinge upon their creativity and ever-increasing desire to write broadly with both conviction and freedom.

Though whole language curricula is designed primarily for younger children, the principles can be useful for effective learning programs for older persons as well. Many of them are endeavoring to increase their level of literacy in a meaningful manner. Some, no doubt, find it difficult to engage in creative writing since they may be afraid to engage in risk-taking with respect to spelling, correct writing form, and sentence structure. To make the older learner comfortable in a whole language environment, teachers need to write and speak with the learner. Lively conversations should take place regarding the views expressed by characters in a fiction selection.

The major force behind an effective whole language curriculum is the fact that the teacher uses a wide range of quality literature on many different subject and ability levels. It provides an avenue whereby learners can construct a broad speaking, writing, and listening vocabulary and provides the motivation to help insure high reading interest levels.

In summary, the following are the most salient features of the whole language program. The whole language teacher believes in certain teaching and learning principles such as the following:

**Children, by and large, have an inherent motivation to learn and desire to try to make sense of the structure of the world about them.**

**Because of the creative nature of the whole language classroom, one will not find two teachers who conduct lessons in the same precise**

manner. The learning needs of the pupils and the basic structure of the school environment dictate that there be a variety of approaches.

The effective whole language teacher places the child and his/her learning needs at the center of instruction. The instructor is the creator of the teaching-learning environment and does not relinquish the role of the teacher in making sure that certain objectives are met.

The whole language teacher is inherently flexible in the creation of lesson strategies and realizes that he/she must expect to defend a teaching model that is not characterized by a strict, rigid adherence to a series of basal readers or a set of workbooks.

The whole language teacher recognizes that accountability is an important part of any school environment and is not afraid to demonstrate that children who are a part of a true whole language environment can compare most favorably with those pupils in a traditional basal reading, workbook setting.

## STRATEGIES FOR IMPLEMENTING
## A WHOLE LANGUAGE CURRICULUM

As noted earlier, whole language is not a precise, sequential new teaching approach but rather a change of attitude with regard to how children learn and how the different language arts are correlated into a meaningful set of learning experiences. Farris and Kaczmarski[8] set the stage for the whole language classroom by noting that reading, writing, mathematics, science, and social studies—the core of the elementary curriculum—need to be on the students' level and relevant if the children are to retain knowledge and apply it in other situations. Developing readers and writers need to be involved in writing events of their own and in reading a wide range of real, comprehensible books. Children must be in control of their reading development.

In light of the basic principles of the philosophy and development of an effective program of whole language instruction, the following is a sample listing of strategies employed by numerous innovative instructors. Each strategy must be evaluated and altered, if necessary, for application of its use for any particular group of learners.

1. For primary-grade children, the wide use of predictable books should be used. The stories should have a suitable background with a logical sequential development of plot that allows the reader to predict the final outcome of the story. Allowances should be made for honest

disagreements among children regarding what they perceive the ending of the story to be. The predictions of the pupils may be mentioned orally or written in a creative, nonthreatening environment. A further alternative would be that of permitting learners to draw or illustrate the final stage of a selection. Pupils may wish to review the story on an audio-tape with their person prediction of the story ending.

2. "Immersion" activities should be used extensively at all learning levels. Teachers should introduce pupils to a large number of literature sources including such items as trade books, Big Books, magazines, and newspapers of both the adult and student varieties. Units or themes may be developed such as "Our Neighborhood" or "Space Travel," and pupils are invited to select stories, articles, plays, and poetry that contribute to the selected theme. With these projects learners are encouraged to read for many purposes, and content area materials such as those found in science and social studies provide the basis for the contextual material of many lessons.

The reading activities associated with these kinds of immersion activities should be constructed to help students become fluent in language as they expand their understanding of numerous text materials. In light of these goals, the California State Board of Education issued guidelines of the *English-Language Arts Framework* in 1987 that emphasizes that schools should promote a systematic literature program with a meaning-centered approach based on intensive reading, writing, speaking, and listening. They believe that an essential part of the movement is language arts instruction through a curriculum that recognizes what we know about how students learn and use language have important implications for how school authorities develop curriculum, select textbooks, and plan programs and activities.

3. Peer writing workshops may be an important aspect of any whole language classroom. With this approach, teams of pupils are challenged to write short selections and/or poems relating to a theme topic. Each learner analyzes the content and structure of his/her peers and suggests appropriate changes or additions to improve the overall body of writing. Pupils may choose to read aloud each selection and reactions solicited from other members of the group.

4. Journal writing can be an exciting and profitable activity. Sandmark and Coon[9] describe this type of strategy in a recent article. The teacher read *The Stupids Step Out* by Harry Allard (Houghton Mifflin, 1974). The family in the story had many silly adventures. Pupils were encour-

aged to think of many unusual adventures that the Stupids might have had that didn't appear in the book. While the motivation was at a high level, the learners were asked to open their journals to the first page. They were asked to draw a picture of the Stupids at the top of the page and save space at the bottom for a sentence that described the nature of the picture. "Invented" spelling was permitted, but it produced mixed feelings in the class. While some students enjoyed the independence of creative spelling, others found it to be troublesome. Those who could not accept the creative spelling philosophy stayed with words that they knew they could spell and wrote in a cautious manner. The result in at least one case was a colorless, unimaginative selection. Another pupil copies only the sentence starter from the board. While writing, he asked often how to spell words correctly even though his teacher reminded him to "try it—and put down the sounds you hear." In all cases the students could use readers and dictionaries as much as they desired.

5. A variety of activities may be instituted to help pupils learn about the nature of language. For the teacher, several principles must be kept in mind:

    a. Whole to parts learning is emphasized and learning begins with the concrete and moves to the abstract.

    b. The theories of "wholesome" is stressed and conforms to the basic structure of gestalt psychology.

    c. Learners learn language for personal reasons and inward forces motivate learning.

    d. Rewards are nonextrinsic in nature and the total body of language is learned through an immersion process.[10]

6. Reading aloud on the part of both the teacher and pupils is an excellent opportunity for the instructor and the learners to share favorite books they have read recently. A reader's theatre provides an excellent opportunity for learning disabled children to rehearse an oral reading selection in preparation for an audience-oriented presentation. The repeated readings along with the added motivation of performance give necessary practice and repetition as well as extra motivation to read.[11]

7. "Word rubberbanding" is an innovative teaching strategy for use with learning disabled pupils who are in a whole language resource classroom. When these learners participate in shared reading experiences, they will begin to relate letters to sounds, and the patterns of language written down. Using this process, the teacher or other children in the

classroom stretch out the sounds of the words much like stretching a rubber band. In the example of the word *man*, the helper would say "mmmmmm—aaaaa—nnnnn, mm-aa-nn, man." From this rubberbanding, the child begins to pay greater attention to the sounds that constitute the words he or she needs to read and spell.[12]

8. Wason-Ellam[13] developed an interesting writing program that stretched across the entire curriculum. The activities were based on the philosophy that writing has two major functions: (1) writing for informing and (2) writing for learning. In a mathematics classroom the program was structured so that students worked at math centers on activities designed to teach meaningful concepts rather than numerical symbols. Inductive problem-solving was promoted in order for students to identify problems and suggest quantitative solutions. The strategies built in the learner a "math sense" which became the basis for further analytic reasoning. Opportunities were presented to the students to put mathematical language into their own words and to speculate on mathematical solutions in their journals. In the final analysis, pupils were asked to interpret and relate what they saw and heard to other parts of their experience. The total program helped learners to experience new relationships among the various language arts in a whole language setting.

9. The *language experience approach* is utilized by many whole language teachers to help children gain the opportunity to see the process through which ideas are translated into text. Among other things, it provides basic information about the technical aspects of writing; demonstrates the planning, drafting, and revision stages of writing; and provides all of the learners with valuable experience in the sustained monologue required in writing.[14] The lessons have a high interest level since they are based on the present unique experiences of children. The dictation of episodes in their lives provides them with the inspiration to speak, write, and read in a creative manner. In instances when a pupil serves as the recorder, the use of invented spelling should be permitted. The whole language teacher is interested in seeing the young child record creative ideas using those graphic symbols that best portray the meaning that he or she intends for an audience. As learners gain more experience as a recorder, they will improve on the basic principles of written work such as proper sentence construction and idea building.

10. Young children in the first grade should be involved in writing activities. Gunderson and Shapiro[15] analyzed the writing sample of two first-grade classes in Vancouver, British Columbia. At the very begin-

ning of school the pupils were asked to write independently in their log books. Several categories of writers were discovered at the beginning of the school year: (1) those who wrote strings of letters; (2) those who wrote strings of letters containing some invented spellings, and (3) those who could write some text, usually with many invented spellings. During the year the teachers provided the pupils with large amounts of interesting literature that required selecting books that matched each student's interests. Students read their own writing and shared writing they did in response to theme assignments. At the end of the year the pupils produced a huge volume of writing and exhibited vocabulary recognition and use that was much higher than if they had been using a basal program. The program activities constituted the first literacy experiences for the young learners and showed them that writing truly represented language and meaning. High frequency word development was dramatic in these whole language classrooms. The inductive teaching methods utilized allowed the students to learn rapidly the mature forms of writing. Gunderson and Shapiro warn teachers that whole language programs are not easy to implement and maintain, but they believe the benefits have only just begun to be discovered.

11. Suzanne Weis of the Omaha, Nebraska Public Schools developed an interesting writing strategy called "A Pattern For Writing."[16] The description follows.

## A Pattern For Writing

Children have wonderful stories to tell. They want to write. From the squiggles made by a tiny tot to the writing on sidewalks or the entries in a diary, children delight in the power of their writing.

Research shows that writing is not haphazard but usually passes through overlapping stages to include Rehearsal, Drafting, Revision, and Editing.

Writing can be taught by writing with your students and sharing the process with them. The writing process includes everything about the topic to the final revisions of the completed paper.

Teachers need not be expert writers to "write" with children. Making a commitment to teach writing offers a chance to grow and to learn with children.

### Rehearsal

The easiest way to begin is to show children how YOU select a topic. Using a large sheet of paper, the overhead projector or a word processor such as FrEdWriter, write down three to four topics and tell about your interest in each. Give them paper and time to do the same. Choose one topic from your list and tell the class what you hope to learn by writing about it. Also, jot down a few notes that you wish to include. Tell the class to select one of their topics and to take a few minutes to tell a friend what they are planning to write.

### Revise/Conferencing

During a writing conference, the writer learns to look again at what has been said and to interact with it. The writing conference provides an audience for the writer. Hold the conferences together at first, modeling questions they will later ask of each other and themselves. For example:

—What is your story about?
—What needs to be fixed?
—What will you do next?
—What part do you like best?

During the conferences, the child does most of the talking. The conference setting offers a good place to model organizing information so that the reader can understand the writer's feelings, grasp the concepts and use the information.

### Make a Rough Draft

Next show the students how YOU compose. Write slowly so the children can see your words, and give the thinking that goes with your writing. Sometimes say, "I don't know what I want to say next. I'll read this aloud to see where I am." At times when reading it aloud, stop and have the children ask questions about what they want to know next. This is modeling questions they can ask each other. Show them that your first concern is content, that it is okay to cross out and keep going, and that misspellings and false starts are part of a rough draft. Give them time to write.

### Edit

The writer double-checks to make sure the rules of language—punctuation, spelling, grammar—are followed so mistakes will not interfere with the message.

Use of the word processor to produce a finished copy often provides incentive to an author. (Reprinted by permission of the author.)

12. Many whole language teachers make use of the computer as an important tool in writing activities. The following is a short essay by Candice Madich regarding this technique.

## Writing and the Computer[17]

Current theory and research in language acquisition look upon the integration of reading and writing as crucial. This clearly suggests that reading and writing should not be taught as discrete units but appear simultaneously in our daily teaching plans. Writing is learned through involvement in the writing process: thoughtful preparations, composing a rough draft, revising and editing, and finally the polished product.

Authors of computer software are attempting to integrate reading and writing as they begin to realize the marketability of software that is in harmony with current educational theory. Thus, use of the microcomputer as a tool in word processing and the writing process is gaining credibility and popularity. A word processing program allows students to take risks when writing, to be experimental about what they may write, correct mistakes with no eraser crumbs, or torn papers, and to see the fruit of their labor in final form without having to hand write multitudinous corrected copies. Following are brief reviews of some available software designed to encourage children in the writing process and suggestions for use:

*Bank Street Writer* by Scholastic is a word processing program allowing the writer to enter and edit text, save text on disks for future use, and produce a printed copy. It allows editing without leaving the original writing screen and can be quite easily used by students at the intermediate level. At the primary level where keyboarding skills are not yet developed, students can dictate language experience sentences and stories as the teacher types. The printed copy is used for reading back what was dictated.

*Missing Links* by Sunburst is a series of programs in which the teacher can enter text (or use prepared text in some versions) to create cloze activities. At the user's command, the program deletes all vowels, all consonants, every other word, etc. from the text, and students must then fill in these deletions to make the text whole again. Because the teacher can enter text, it is suitable for any grade level.

*Magic Slate* by Sunburst provides three different letter sizes for ease of reading from the monitor: standard type, primary type, and an in-between size. It also prints out in the three type sizes. The large print option makes it especially useful for primary children and for groups gathered around the computer dictating a story as their teacher types. Individual students composing with *Magic Slate* might be seen entering stories with titles such as "My Best Birthday Present" or "The Time I Got My Stitches."

*Story Maker* by Scholastic enables students to create and print stories with illustrations. There are eight different typestyles available, and illustrations are added to stories by choosing from a variety of ready-made pictures built into the program, at the screen. The student chooses where on the page each illustration will be placed. Stories of any length, from one sentence to several chapters, can be created and printed. It is suitable for the elementary and junior high levels. *Story Maker* is especially useful as students compose book reports. A favorite part of the book could be summarized and illustrated.

*Microzine* programs by Scholastic provide a variety of writing opportunities. Examples of guided writing activities are: letter-writing, creating a mininewspaper, completion of cartoon strips, and making entries in a journal. Most programs are designed for ages 9 and above.

*Kidwriter* by Spinnaker (ages 6–10) allows children to create pictures and write a related story. Picture story pages may be linked together to create story books of many pages. Pictures are created using objects chosen from a prepared gallery of 99 available objects. Typing is simplified, because like many word processors, if a word won't fit on a line, the program will put the whole word on the next line for the child. Because the features of the program are easy to manipulate, *Kidwriter* is especially useful in a peer-tutor situation. In one classroom, a group of first graders is working with sixth grade tutors. First graders write and illustrate stories with the help of their tutor; later first graders dictate their completed stories as tutors type. Illustrations are added using the available objects.

---

Word processing by students gives a dimension of excitement to composing that is not possible with pencil and paper. As a teacher, your role in the writing process is crucial. Remember to evaluate with encouraging remarks and constructive criticism only. Keep in mind that the process is as important as the product!
(Reprinted by permission of the author.)

13. Whole language classrooms are quickly identified by the quality and quantity of complete stories that are listened to, read, written, and shared. When children listen to stories they are learning how language works, how text is composed, and how ideas can be put together to create meaning. A developmental listening program can be instituted that consists of three fundamental stages: prelistening, focused listening, and postlistening.[18]

In the prelistening stage, pupils are motivated to focus their listening for the story about to be read. During focussed listening the teacher emphasizes the importance of such aspects as intonation and nonverbal cues to assist meaning. The teacher should practice the stories so that the learners can give full attention to oral expression and fluent reading. Postlistening involves the use of questions for oral discussion to help link the developmental strand of the listening focus with the story schema.

## EVALUATING THE EFFECTS OF WHOLE LANGUAGE INSTRUCTION

As with any kind of reading instruction program, a careful evaluation instrument should be considered to determine the overall effect of teaching strategies on the cognitive and affective skill components with respect to each learner. There are numerous methods and procedures that may be utilized. Bill Harp[19] notes that according to Turbill, writing may be evaluated by at least four methods: (1) subjective and impressionistic means that reside in the teacher's head; (2) use of an anecdotal record book or profile of day-to-day observations; (3) examining pupil's writing folder to look for patterns emerging over time; (4) completion of a writing folder by the learner entitled "Things I Have Learned." He notes that schools are moving increasingly to a holistic evaluation of writing performance.

The evaluation criteria used for evaluating whole language is increasingly more process focussed. Instead of concentrating on "grade scores" or "instructional reading levels," whole language teachers are more concerned with such aspects as children's interests, level of functioning, and stage of literacy development. Miscue analysis is one important strategy for analyzing the cueing systems developed by the pupil.[20]

While cognitive skill components should receive proper evaluation, a careful analysis should be made with regard to such affective items as willingness to read, selecting books independently, reads a wide variety of materials, uses meaning clues, exhibits good self-concept about reading, demonstrates basic comprehension skills, and reads independently for information and pleasure. Observing pupils at work with their attendant commitment to reading will reveal much valuable data. Their conversations concerning reading interests and attitudes will yield many insights regarding the types and kinds of reading strategies that should be used. Additional suggestions for evaluating the reading competencies of all types of learners can be found in Chapter VIII.

## SUMMARY

Whole language instruction is a very valuable strategy for teaching and integrating a total program of language arts. While it has been used in Australia and New Zealand for many years, it is now being used extensively in many parts of the United States.

As noted in this chapter, there are many principles of whole language instruction that should be observed. There are distinct and contrasting differences that can be made with traditional basal approaches. It is a philosophical and instructional philosophy that promotes the idea that most pupils are inherently eager to learn and read if they are placed in a relaxed, nonthreatening atmosphere where they can engage in reading risk-taking and invented spelling.

The many teaching suggestions for promoting whole language development can be adapted to accommodate any pupil at any learning level. A program of appropriate evaluation will serve to help the teacher decide if certain strategies are proper for a given group of pupils.

## REFERENCES

1. Goodman, Ken. *What's Whole In Whole Language?* Portsmouth, New Hampshire, Heinemann, 1986, p. 7.
2. Carter, Susan H. "Ask The Teacher," *Omaha World-Herald,* August 28, 1988.
3. Farris, Pamela J. and Debra Kaczmarski, "Whole Language, A Closer Look," *Contemporary Education,* Vol. 59, No. 2 (Winter, 1988), p. 78.
4. Newman, Judith M. *Whole Language Theory In Use.* Portsmouth, New Hampshire, Heinemann, 1985, p. 28.
5. Farris and Kaczmarski, p. 79.
6. Berglund, Roberta L., "A Swing of The Pendulum or A Whole New Pendulum?" *Reading Today,* Vol. 6, No. 3 (December 1988/January 1989), p. 18.
7. Newman, p. 13.
8. Farris, Pamela J. and Debra Kaczmarski, "Whole Language, A Closer Look," *Contemporary Education,* Vol. 59, No. 2 (Winter, 1988), p. 78.
9. Sandmark, Laura and George E. Coon, "Learning To Read by Writing about Reading," *Teaching K-8,* Vol. 18, No. 6 (March, 1988), pp. 60–61.
10. Reutzel, D. Ray and Paul M. Hollingsworth, "Whole Language and The Practitioner," *Academic Therapy,* Vol. 23, No. 4 (March, 1988), pp. 413–414.
11. Hollingsworth, Paul M. and D. Ray Reutzel, "Whole Language With LD Children," *Academic Therapy,* Vol. 23, No. 5 (May, 1988), p. 483.
12. Hollingsworth and Reutzel, p. 484.
13. Wason-Ellam, Linda, "Writing Across The Curriculum," *Canadian Journal of English Language Arts,* Vol. 11, No. 3 (Fall, 1987), pp. 5–7.
14. Shanahan, Timothy, "The Reading-Writing Relationship," *Reading Teacher,* Vol. 41, No. 7 (March, 1988), p. 639.
15. Gunderson, Lee and Jon Shapiro, "Whole Language Instruction: Writing In 1st Grade," *Reading Teacher,* Vol. 41, No. 4 (January, 1988), pp. 430–437.
16. Weis, Suzanne, "A Pattern For Writing," *Collage,* Vol. 12, No. 1 (May, 1987), p. 5. (Reprinted by permission of the author.)

17. Madich, Candace, "Writing And The Computer," *Collage*, Vol. 12, No. 1 (May, 1987), pp. 16–17. (Reprinted by permission of the author.)
18. Craddock, Sonja and Honey Halpern, "Developmental Listening In A Whole Language Classroom," *Canadian Journal of English Language Arts*, Vol. 11, No. 1 (1988), pp. 19–22.
19. Harp, Bill, "When The Principal Asks," *Reading Teacher*, Vol. 42, No. 2 (November, 1988), p. 160.
20. Harp, p. 161.

## Chapter IV

# DEVELOPING WORD ATTACK SKILLS

Regardless of the methodology used to teach reading skills, it is the opinion of numerous reading specialists that concentrated attention should be given to the promotion of a well-devised program of skill development in the area of word attack. The versatile reader must possess demonstrated proficiency in the ability to utilize numerous techniques for unlocking words. Many members of the lay public are convinced that the lack of appropriate instruction in phonics is the central reason why some learners fail to read properly. Word analysis is to the reading process what the heart is to the human anatomy. The completion of the reading process of word analysis is necessary before the reading product of comprehension can be realized.

This chapter is designed to supply important information relating to four significant segments of reading instruction relating to word attack development. They are: place of word attack skills; principles for teaching word attack skills; development of word attack competencies; and evaluating word attack proficiency.

## PLACE OF WORD ATTACK SKILLS

From a teaching-learning standpoint, one of the most difficult tasks a pupil has to accomplish is identifying the printed symbol that stands for the spoken sound. Though most kindergarten children from average socioeconomic backgrounds can speak hundreds of words, they may have much difficulty identifying these words when they are in written form. The task becomes even more difficult when they discover there is not a perfect phoneme-grapheme relationship in the English language. Because of these conditions it is necessary for teachers to establish an appropriate instructional program that will provide the pupil with those skills necessary for his/her later success in undertaking the reading act.

To become an able reader, the learner must develop the ability to use a number of word attack strategies such as phonetic analysis, structural analysis, dictionary, and context clues. The emphasis on phonics usually occurs at the primary grade levels with additional attention given to the use of structural analysis, context clues, and dictionary skills at the middle grade levels. The emphasis on each of these skills depends on a number of facets including the learning levels of the pupils and the reading tasks they are asked to perform.

Not all skills for identifying words are necessarily taught within the school environment. Alert children learn many sight words that are a part of their neighborhood environment such as *park, motel,* and *McDonald's.* Pupils that have had the good fortune to have parents and/or grandparents read to them are able to establish the phoneme-grapheme relationship much easier than those who have not had such experiences.

According to Karlin and Karlin[1] frequent exposure of words in a variety of meaning contexts is of considerable value in helping pupils learn an ever growing number of sight words. Children who learn to recognize many words are more relaxed to think about the ideas they take from and bring to printed materials. The final goal of any reading curriculum is to reduce to the minimum the amount and kinds of words they must study carefully.

In deciding to teach certain new words to young children, one must keep in mind that they should already be a part of their oral vocabulary. A child who instantly recognizes many words is likely to be skillful at recognizing words he or she does not instantly recognize; and a child who has well-developed techniques for understanding words is likely to recognize many words instantly.[2]

## PRINCIPLES FOR TEACHING WORD ATTACK SKILLS

There are several important principles to remember when building a word attack program. If these are integrated and made a part of the everyday teaching plans of all teachers, the ability to unlock and pronounce a large number of unknown words becomes much easier.

1. **The first major decision of a teacher in a word attack program is to decide as carefully as possible what word analysis competencies need to be mastered by a group of pupils.** The date used for selecting appropriate skill components may come from a variety of sources such as the established curriculum or basal program adopted by the school. In states where competency tests are required, the word attack program may be constructed to emphasize these components. In a whole language class-

room, the teacher may base the skills competencies needed on the observed needs of individual pupils. Strategy skill sessions could be scheduled on an "as needed" basis during a designated period during the school day.

In those instances when a teacher's competency is geared to pupil achievement test performance, the goals of instruction may be necessarily correlated to the required items on the test. **In every instance, the day-to-day instructional programs must always relate to the individual needs of the learners.**

2. **A carefully devised program of evaluation for word attack skills must be constructed.** There are a number of diagnostic tests of both the commercial and teacher-made types that may be used. (Chapter VIII contains a description of many different evaluative instruments that may be used.) Effective informal strategies may include such instruments as the subjective reading inventory, cloze test, and oral reading experiences. While reading aloud the teacher should use appropriate symbols to designate miscues such as omissions, substitutions, and repetitions.

To carefully analyze the strengths and limitations of each learner in decoding skills, the teacher should construct a profile sheet with the names on the left side of the sheet and the list of desired competencies in vertical columns. One could determine a desired criterion performance for each skill and make a check beside the names of the students who need further work. Small groups of students who need similar instruction could be placed together in scheduled strategy improvement sessions for the purpose of upgrading such components as phonetic and structural analysis and dictionary skills.

3. **Teachers should use every available technique to motivate each pupil to increase his or her level of word attack proficiency.** Pupil-teacher conferences should be held during which time the instructor points out the *present* achievement levels of the learner and challenges the pupil to attempt even higher levels of proficiency. One of the methods of achieving this goal would be to have the affected learner listen to an audiotape of his/her oral reading and thus analyze any mistakes made in word decoding in the privacy of an individual conference. Teacher-made goal sheets for learning a certain number of new words may also prove to be motivating.

4. **Procedures should be initiated to help pupils gain as much success as possible in a brief period of time.** The first step in the process is to find the *present* level of competency for each student in each of the major word attack skill areas. The lessons could be of a concentrated nature and constructed to promote one definitive skill. Such a lesson may be the

processes involved in dividing words and the meaning and importance of Latin prefixes and suffixes. Presentations should be made that utilize a wide variety of teaching tools such as the overhead projector, skill sheet components, and computer software.

5. **Meaningful practice should be given to students after they have mastered a word analysis skill.** Pupils should have ample opportunities provided that will allow them to practice the skill in a natural content subject environment. If, for example, the meaning and significance of Latin prefixes and suffixes has been presented, it is very important to introduce numerous new words at the beginning of a lesson in order for learners to grasp the meanings in their natural settings. Creative writing activities may also be instituted. Various words used in the writing can be analyzed for such aspects as syllabic division, vowel digraphs, blends, root words, and compound words.

6. **Teaching strategies used for word attack should be evaluated on both a periodic and continuous basis to determine if the instructional plans are accomplishing their desired goals.** There are numerous evaluative measures available for measuring the effectiveness of teaching techniques. One of the most useful of all the approaches is simply the listening of a given child engaging in oral reading and/or analyzing a pupil's responses given on a pencil and paper test constructed by the teacher. For example, one may wish to administer a multiple-choice test involving a list of words with varying numbers of syllables. The learner chooses the answer that denotes the correct way of dividing a given word. Commercial tests can be given such as the *Doren Diagnostic Reading Test* (group) or the *Durrell Analysis of Reading Difficulty* (individual diagnostic). In using any and all types of evaluative tools, the student's proficiency on such instruments should be discussed with the child in an individual conference. An increasing awareness of the value of self-diagnosis and evaluation should be stressed continuously. Small group critiques of peer performance may be useful in certain situations if the right environment is present. All data secured from evaluative measures must always be used to measure the degree to which the teaching objectives have been met.

## IMPORTANT CONCEPTS FOR
## TEACHING WORD ATTACK SKILLS

Many reading educators perceive the ability to analyze or pronounce words correctly as the core or heart of the reading act. As Simms and

Falcon[3] note, "In order to be effective readers, children must be proficient in word recognition skills; they cannot stop to analyze every word they encounter and at the same time read fluently." Pupils in all types of classrooms (including whole language) must become independent word analyzers and be able to use phonic and contextual clues with much facility. Young children need to be presented with a well-designed phonics program. Though most children today are taught phonics, often the instruction is poorly conceived. Phonics, for example, is more likely to be useful when children hear the sounds associated with most letters both in isolation and in words and when they are taught to blend together the sounds of letters to identify words.[4]

To establish a useful program of word attack demands the consideration of a list of principles that will help insure a level of maximum learning for all children. The following list is practical and relevant for teachers with varying levels of teaching experience and available resources. They are not placed in any particular order of importance and each should be considered of equal relevance.

1. **Though phonic analysis is useful as a tool for unlocking as many as 86 percent of the words in the English language, it should be stressed that it should be used in a natural setting and is only one strategy available to readers.** Incorporating phonics instruction into the teaching of reading continues to be a controversial subject. Those who oppose its incorporation note the inconsistency of sound-symbol relationship in the English language. While phonic opponents favor reading instruction which emphasizes getting meaning from print, those who advocate phonics favor reading methods which emphasize "breaking the code."[5]

Phonics has been at the center of heated educational debate since the late 1800s. Some teachers conducted phonics drills and insisted that pupils memorize isolated sounds related to letters and letter groups. Presently, most reading educators believe that a systematic approach to phonics at the primary levels is of much help for reading and spelling achievement but should be taught as individually as possible to maximize reading growth.

Fortunately, phonetic analysis instruction has moved away from isolated, meaningless drill and now encompasses the practical teaching of phonics that relate to specific words that pupils meet in their everyday reading. In a whole language environment, these strategy lessons are designed for the unique needs of the learners involved. In summary, phonic analysis is a demonstrated and essential reading skill; it is but one of a number of ways a pupil may "solve" words not known as sight words; and no one process of word attack, such as phonics, is sufficient to meet the reading needs of *all* pupils.

Rod Maclean[6] made an exhaustive study of the relative benefits of phonics instruction and concluded that for a substantial number of children—those who do not spontaneously learn phonic strategies through exposure to print—the teaching of phonics can be beneficial. He cautions about the way phonics is taught. If phonics is an instructional representation, then it does not teach children the rules they will actually use in reading words, but merely puts them in a position to work out their own rules. Therefore, phonics should be seen only as a way of getting children started on the path of learning to read, not as an ongoing teaching strategy. Phonics is merely a catalyst that triggers the process of learning to read. The catalyst will, however, only produce a reaction when it accompanies large amounts of interesting and meaningful reading.

There is a considerable amount of emphasis given by some teachers to the exact memorization of phonic terms and rules. A recent study by Moore and Litcher[7] produced the conclusion that when teaching reading to students, the critical emphasis needs to be on knowledge of phonics usage, instead of memorization of phonics terms. Phonics skills can be learned as isolated subskills, but must be immediately practiced in actual reading. Teachers can best assist in the development of successful readers by providing students with large amounts of interesting reading material and encouragement to read.

2. **One of the broad goals of word-recognition instruction is to help pupils to associate meanings with printed and spoken words.**[8] Reading is much more than the mere pronunciation of words. Unless the reader generates some meaning or understanding regarding the word, he or she has not completed the reading act. Pupils with deficient experience backgrounds with associated impoverished home conditions often have a considerable amount of difficulty with associating meaning with words. Teachers then are obliged to engage in intensive activities involving the use of word cards and language experience activities to strengthen each learner's capability to correlate meaning with word pronunciation. Many of the words learned are sight words that are memorized and recalled after seeing them repeated in many meaningful contexts. Words such as "and," "the," and "teacher" don't have to be memorized because they are a natural part of most learner's daily oral and written language. The

word and meaning associations are constructed at an early age for many children. They see "the golden arches" and immediately associate the word "McDonald's" with hamburgers. The development of a large body of sight words enables the learner to use context clues in a number of sentence settings. These skills then allow the reader the use of structural analysis that provide for the analysis of words into meaningful word elements such as the prefix, suffix, and root word.

3. **An effective reading program of word analysis is characterized by a balanced decoding approach that includes phonics, structural analysis, context clues, sight words and the use of the dictionary.** Stoodt[9] is of the belief that programs that overemphasize one approach to decoding words, while neglecting others, can cause difficulty for students. For instance, overemphasizing sight words and context clues create readers who are dependent on teachers for assistance. If phonics is stressed too much, pupils may become slow and overly analytic readers. In most situations a combined approach is necessary to decode a word. For instance, if the reader encounters the word, *"unfaithful,"* he or she notes the prefix "un," the root word "faith" and the suffix, "ful." Phonics principles can be applied to the root word by establishing the regular sound of the consonant "f" and the elements of the vowel digraph "ai" to reflect the principle of the long sound of "a" and the silent "i."

The dictionary is a useful companion tool when applying the usual phonic principles. Various meanings for each word supply the learner with the most appropriate choices for contextual learning. Graded volumes are especially valuable since they allow for the expected sequential learning levels of pupils at various grade levels.

4. **Independence in word attack should be a sought-after goal by every learner.** A thorough training in the use of combined strategies allows the child to at least attempt the pronunciation of a word that is unfamiliar. An atmosphere should be developed that is nonthreatening and risk taking is possible. A whole language classroom is ideal since the pupil is encouraged to attempt the speaking and/or writing of a word if it is "invented" and not correct according to current spelling and grammar rules.

Peer tutoring and cooperative learning (as described later in this volume) are two important strategies for promoting independence. Suitable computer-assisted tutorial lessons are also valuable. Practice given to pupils to help them develop self-appraisal skills will help them determine when they need further practice and/or remediation to improve their overall level of reading achievement.

# DEVELOPMENT OF WORD ATTACK COMPETENCIES

A careful study of the scope and sequence organizational structures of various basal programs and other instructional strategies reveals a wide divergence of opinion regarding the sequential structure that should be followed. Reading skills should be taught in sequence whenever a hierarchy can be detected.

The curriculum for word attack that should be established must be based on a number of different factors such as the age and learning level of the learner, mental and social development, and instructional objectives. A study of the scope and sequence charts related to various basal reading series reveals a great disparity regarding the precise time when skills should be introduced, taught, and reinforced. *When* a child should learn a skill should be based on *need* rather than a structural, detailed list. In the whole language classroom, ad hoc strategy sessions may be established for those pupils who need certain word attack skills development. The membership of the groups may fluctuate considerably depending on the strengths and limitations of each learner. For example, there may be four third-grade pupils who need additional practice relating to long vowel sounds while another group of six readers may need practice in dividing words into prefixes, root words, and suffixes. Standard lessons emphasizing detailed drillwork on phonic "rules" for a total class cannot be justified in most instances. The rate and kind of lessons presented must always be based on student need as revealed by the data obtained from commercial tests, informal instruments, and careful observation.

For most pupils, the following general sequence or structure seems to be appropriate for the skill development from the first through the fourth grades.

## A. Phonic Elements

1. Single consonants and their sounds in various locations in a word or phrase.
2. Consonant blend sounds in different words and phrases.
3. Consonant digraph sounds found in various sections of a word.
4. Soft and hard sounds of the letters "c" and "g" (cat, cell, get, gel).
5. Effect of silent letters in consonant combinations (kn, gn).
6. Names of vowels and examples of words with certain vowels.

7. Short and long vowel sounds.
8. Vowels that are influenced by certain letters such as "r," "l," and "w."
9. Sounds of vowel digraphs (ec, oa, oo) and dipthongs (oi, oy, ou).
10. Various word families (all, ute).

## B. Structural Analysis

1. Numerous word endings (est, ing).
2. Nature of common compounds words (grandmother, peanut).
3. Root or base words (un*faith*ful, ex*haust*ed).
4. Useful contractions (isn't, I've, I'm).
5. Possessives and their use (Norma's coat).
6. Meaning and nature of certain prefixes (un, dis, mis, re).
7. Common suffixes and their meanings (less, ness, ly, ful).

## C. Syllabication

1. Knows syllabication generalizations such as the following:
   a. Every syllable has a vowel or vowel sound.
   b. If a word contains a prefix and a root word, the word is normally divided between these two meaning units.
   c. If the first vowel letter in a word is followed by two consonant letters, the first syllable normally terminates with the first of the two consonants.
   d. If the first vowel letter is followed by a single consonant letter, the consonant usually begins the second syllable.
   e. If the first vowel element is followed by a two-letter consonant symbol (sh, th) this symbol remains intact when the word is divided into syllables.
   f. When the first vowel element of a word is followed by a consonant blend, the blend often begins the second syllable.

Recommendations concerning the teaching of phonic generalizations were discussed earlier. **The following are some general recommendations for teaching structural analysis and syllabication skills to elementary children of all age and learning levels.**

**Avoid the temptation to recommend the procedure for finding small words in larger words.** If words are regular in a compound structure, it is satisfactory to use the procedure (e.g., grandmother). Unfortunately, there are large numbers of words that don't conform to this practice and those prove to be hazardous such as in the words "maple" and "father." Trying to divide the word "breakfast" into *break* and *fast* can also prove to be difficult.

**Always help pupils analyze "strange" words in a meaningful context rather than in an isolated list.** The child may discover that context clues provide an important adjunct in the recognition and understanding of unfamiliar words. There are numerous words in the English language that are pronounced differently depending on their location in a sentence (read, refuse). **Readers should understand that other word attack strategies may be more useful than structural analysis on some occasions.** Context clues and phonetic analysis may be more appropriate for application to strange words. A child should never be given the impression that it is necessary to note all of the words by locating meaning units.

**The inductive approach should be used when teaching structural analysis principles.** Situations should be presented that are illustrative of the principle to be taught. For example, the teacher may desire to teach the generalization that when the first vowel letter in a word is followed by two consonant letters, the first syllable usually ends with the first of the two consonants. Placing the words "matter" and "latter" on the greenboard would help the child to discover this generalization.

## EVALUATING WORD ATTACK PROFICIENCY

To build an effective word attack program for pupils, both individually and collectively, requires the use of a broad spectrum of *commercial* and *informal* devices and strategies. These are described in the following section along with the names of appropriate examples. (For a complete description of a reading evaluation program, see Chapter VIII.)

### Commercial Tests

Under this title, one may find three major types of instruments: *end-of-level basal reader tests*, *standardized achievement tests*, and *competency tests*. All of these instruments measure various types of reading skills including word attack, comprehension, vocabulary, and study skills. Standardized tests are commonly described as *norm-referenced* because the test constructors have utilized the performance scores of hundreds of pupils in various locations for the norm groups. In many instances the publisher offers local, state, and national norms as well as computer scoring of the answer sheets. Teachers can request from the publisher multiple kinds of scores—for instance, raw scores, percentile ranks, stanines, and grade equivalents, all of which are defined in the test manuals.[10]

*Criterion-referenced tests* are inherently competency-based because the constructor determines in advance the number of items that must be answered correctly if mastery is to be ascertained. For example, a test is given to a student that contains a list of thirty words with varying numbers of syllables. The pupil is asked to write the number of syllables each word has. If he or she gets twenty-seven or more, "mastery" is thought to have been achieved. Several years ago such tests gained a wide level of recognition and importance since they were used to individual mastery of huge numbers of discrete reading skills such as those in the *Wisconsin Design* and similar programs.

## Teacher-Made Tests

There are various types of teacher devised instruments that are uniquely designed to measure word attack skill competency. These include the use of the subjective reading inventory for evaluating the correct pronunciation of words through the oral reading of familiar passages; the cloze test for determining context clue efficiency, and specific practice tests for studying a child's approach to syllabication.

When using all of these types of tests the teacher may be seeking answers to a number of specific questions such as the following:

1.  Do the students exhibit the ability to identify words independently and with ease?
2.  Do they demonstrate an undue overdependence on any one approach such as phonics?
3.  Is it evident what strategies they may be using for decoding long and complex words and phrases?
4.  Do they have knowledge of a sufficient stock of sight words to allow them to pronounce a long list of common words?
5.  Are they sufficiently skilled in word attack competencies so they will avoid the temptation to omit difficult words or solicit undue assistance from a teacher or peer?

In summarizing the use, importance, and nature of reading tests, Dr. Roger Farr[11] offers a number of important suggestions for teachers to follow when they consider the importance they should attach to the results from reading tests. They are:

**Never use reading tests as the sole criterion for judging the quality of an educational program.**

**Reading assessment tests are often misunderstood and misused and they are not as good as they can be.**

**Basal reader level tests and other standardized reading tests often measure reading as if it were a set of discrete skills.**

**A promising movement in the reading assessment scene is an attempt to assess the reading process rather than just the reading result.**

**When we select reading accountability tests we should find those that provide scores about what learners can do; how they read; and assess reading as a purposeful behavior.**

## SUMMARY

The ability to identify, decode, and analyze words is a central competency that must be developed by all pupils. There are numerous principles that should be considered by all teachers as they help learners enlarge their competencies in this area.

There is some general agreement among reading program developers regarding the overall sequence of development. The sequence has been described in this chapter. Those teachers using the whole language approach will abide by a less structured sequence and provide word attack strategy lessons based on student need.

The instructional program to follow must be constructed after a careful analysis is made of each pupil's **present reading** abilities. As noted by Dr. Farr, a number of aspects should be considered in addition to the sole attention given to a single reading score such as a grade placement or percentile figure.

## REFERENCES

1. Karlin, Robert and Andrea R. Karlin. *Teaching Elementary Reading Principles and Strategies* (Fourth Edition). New York, Harcourt Brace Jovanovich, 1987, pp. 192–193.
2. Finn, Patrick J. *Helping Children Learn To Read.* New York, Random House, 1985, p. 64.

3. Simms, Rochelle B. and Susan Claire Falcon, "Teaching Sight Words," *Teaching Exceptional Children*, Vol. 20, No. 1 (Fall, 1987), p. 30.

4. Commission on Reading. *Becoming A Nation of Readers: The Report of the Commission On Reading.* Washington, U.S. Department of Education, 1984, p. 118.

5. Johnson, Barbara and Linda Hehnert, "Learning Phonics Naturally: A Model For Instruction," *Reading Horizons* Vol. 24, No. 2 (Winter, 1984), p. 90.

6. Maclean, Rod, "Two Paradoxes of Phonics," *The Reading Teacher,* Vol. 41, No. 6 (February, 1988), pp. 516–517.

7. Moore, Lynn J. and John H. Litcher, "A Comparison of Children's Ability to Define and Apply Phonics Terms," *Reading Horizons,* Vol. 23, No. 1 (Fall, 1983), p. 31.

8. Stoodt, Barbara D. *Reading Instruction* (Second Edition). New York, Harper & Row, 1989, p. 120.

9. Stoodt, pp. 125–126.

10. Durkin, Dolores. *Teaching Them To Read* (Fifth Edition). Boston, Allyn and Bacon, 1989, p. 487.

11. Farr, Roger, "New Trends in Reading Assessment: Better Tests, Better Uses," *Curriculum Review,* Vol. 27, No. 1 (September–October, 1987), p. 22.

## Chapter V

# INCREASING COMPREHENSION ABILITIES

Many reading authorities consider the ability to comprehend printed material to be the end product or the ultimate goal of the act of reading. As noted in the previous chapter, word identification constitutes the heart of any successful reading endeavor; however, the reading act is not completed until the learner has received the intended message supplied by the writer. One of the primary goals of any effective program of instruction should be that of developing readers who have a total understanding of what they read along with an attendant mode of personal reaction to the message.

While there is a movement among some educators to consider comprehension in a holistic manner, there appears to be some definable skill segments at the literal, interpretive, critical, and creative levels. If the ability to derive meaning from the printed page is to be realized, numerous factors or considerations must be considered. These include such aspects as the learner's background of experience, basic word attack ability, and purposes for reading. The reading success that any elementary pupil may realize in a school environment appears to be significantly correlated with his/her ability to comprehend the seemingly endless amount of printed text materials that are assigned by teachers and administrators. Special emphasis should be given to *all* four levels of comprehension. Unfortunately, too many elementary teachers emphasize the literal and interpretive levels with much lesser attention given to the critical and creative levels.

The purpose of this chapter is to provide specific information and meaningful discussion relating to four important aspects of the total process of developing comprehension. These topics are the meaning of comprehension: factors that influence comprehension ability; the comprehension skill levels; and teaching procedures for building effective understanding.

# THE MEANING OF COMPREHENSION

Two of the most difficult tasks a child is asked to undertake in a school setting are (1) to identify the printed symbols that represent a spoken sound, and (2) derive an appropriate level of understanding relating to what the printed symbols mean. Generally, an alert young child with an average background of experience comes to the kindergarten or first grade classroom speaking dozens of words. The teacher initiates an aggressive instructional program to provide him/her with the skills to decode the words; however, as noted earlier, the reading act is still not complete. The young pupil must not only pronounce the word silently or orally, but also must realize and comprehend the *meaning* of the words and phrases. The learner's ability to comprehend is usually judged by the responses given to oral and written questions.

While teachers should be concerned about the quality and nature of the comprehension product, it is the view of Gray[1] that more concern should be given to the *process*. If comprehension is viewed as a product, instructors cannot be sure of whether a pupil simply did not understand a passage because of the lack of prior knowledge, not making use of prior knowledge possessed, or using inadequate or inappropriate strategies. The only way to investigate the process is to attempt to measure a learner's comprehension monitoring strategies. In all cases teachers must understand that there may be more than a single correct answer to a given question.

Recent research studies in the area of comprehension reveal a significant body of data relating to the meaning of comprehension and how elementary teachers can help insure that their pupils achieve maximum success in deriving understanding of the writer's printed message.

1. **Schema theory that relates to a reader's breadth of understanding regarding a particular subject must be considered as an important factor relating to the degree of competency obtained in comprehending all types of print media.** The nature of the schemata deals with all of the concepts, ideas, and attitudes possessed by the learner as he/she encounters new ideas. Clary[2] notes that this theory reinforces the idea that teachers must give added time to background development and exploration before reading, rather than skimming over that section of their basal lesson plans. It is also important to encourage children to make their own individual predictions before reading and share them with the group.

2. **Comprehension is much more than a culmination of a large body of**

**finite skills.** Meaning is derived when complex processing of both background and reader expectations are carefully integrated. While most readers do, in fact, progress from the literal and interpretive levels to the more critical stages, a few more gifted learners are able to deal with more difficult material such as propaganda techniques at the very early stages of reading development. Through a process of story mapping, pupils may have an infinite knowledge of the relationships among and between various segments and concepts of a selection. Teachers using the Madeline Hunter model of anticipatory set can raise pupils' levels of what they may expect to learn from a body of printed material.

3. **There is no one approach, technique, or strategy that can appraise precisely the level of comprehension competency of any given learner.** Typical standardized achievement tests attempt to measure a learner's proficiency in the general area of comprehension, however there are several affective skill components that are difficult to measure by any type of pencil-and-paper instrument. The attitudes of a learner regarding interest and sensitivity issues in the area must be measured through the use of a variety of commercial and informal devices. Even some cognitive skill segments are difficult to measure. Most prepared tests emphasize one's proficiency in remembering a long list of infinite details that can be utilized as answers in a series of multiple choice items following a short narrative in the test. Rarely do the instruments contain test items measuring critical and creative aspects. Oral questioning and careful observation are required to obtain this information.

Particular attention should be given to each pupil's ability to read "between the lines," discover propaganda techniques, and differentiate between fact and opinion. A grid sheet could be constructed that lists desired competencies vertically at the top of the sheet with pupils' names listed horizontally at the left of the sheet. An "X" could be placed in each box when the results of various evaluative devices appear to suggest that competency has been obtained. Tutorial programs involving both traditional and computer materials may be utilized on an individual basis for those pupils who need specific reinforcement of certain comprehension skills.

4. **Appropriate background information should be supplied for each pupil before they attempt to try to comprehend particular facts and concepts from a narrative and/or factual selection.** To incorporate this concept in a teaching mode requires the instructor to select important concepts, principles, and vocabulary that should be taught and under-

stood previous to the introduction of a lesson or selection. A graphic design may be constructed to give the learners an idea of the sequence of events that are about to be presented. Adequate emphasis should be given to the participatory learning set with sufficient attention given to what incidents or situations may be anticipated. A very important element is that of providing learners with the *purposes* for reading. If details are to be remembered, a slow, deliberate rate should be used, whereas the acquisition of the main idea or theme of the selection may be gained through the use of skimming and scanning techniques.

5. **Data from some studies appear to suggest that having children retell stories in their own words can be very informative.** It eliminates the necessity for questions and can be very enlightening as to the child's interpretations that relate to the youngster's different background that may not come out as clearly through questioning. To do this, we simply ask them to tell us, in their own words, what the passage said.[3] The recollection processes also has the effect of reinforcing various important events and how the incidents were related to the total story theme. The oral reporting of each child provides important clues to each pupil regarding the syntactical and semantic structures of the selection. Additionally, the teacher may invite pupils to suggest ways how the outcome of the story might have been different. These activities may be in either oral or written form.

6. **Comprehension can only be strengthened by providing each pupil with a variety of opportunities to read dozens of books and articles relating to many different topics.** While textbooks and similar materials provide most of the source material for students' comprehension practice, teachers should make a special effort to secure many types of fiction and nonfiction books for pupils to gain practice in such important areas and reading to secure main ideas, identify propaganda techniques, and note the author's purpose.

7. **One of the important strategies for teachers to use in building comprehension skill competencies with pupils of all ability levels is to be sure that each has a distinct purpose for reading.** It is not enough to merely say "Read the story and we will talk about it." An assignment of this type lends no distinct direction to the reader. The typical learner makes a feeble attempt to try to remember a myriad of unimportant details which may or may not be significant. Even at the primary level, pupils need to be challenged with questions that force them to read and think beyond the literal level. One might ask a question such as "Read the next page

and find out what Billy did to make his grandmother happy. What are some ways that *you* use to make your mother or grandmother happy?" Unfortunately, too many teachers are uneasy about asking critical and creative questions since these types of questions cannot be evaluated quickly by objective test single-answer responses.

8. **The materials used for comprehension skills building should be at the instructional reading level of the pupil.** The *estimated* readability of each material should be determined through the use of one or more of the widely used formulae such as the Fry, Dale-Chall, Flesch, and Raygor. These data can be derived by using appropriate computer software. The printer on many computers can deliver the estimated readability level from as many as seven different formulae while considering a series of one hundred word passages that have been processed.

After determining the approximate readability level, the instructional reading level of each pupil can be determined. At this level the elementary student is able to pronounce at least 95 percent of the words when reading aloud and demonstrates an overall comprehension proficiency of at least 75 percent while reading silently. As noted earlier, teachers should have a wide variety of materials available to meet the instructional needs of the learners who have a multiplicity of reading levels. In a typical elementary classroom, one can use the formula *two-thirds times the M.C.A.* (*mean chronological age*) of the pupils to learn the approximate range of reading levels that may be present in any given classroom.

For example, in a sixth-grade class where the M.C.A. may be twelve, one may well find as many as eight different reading levels present. Perhaps a few pupils may be reading as low as the second-grade level while other gifted readers may demonstrate reading competency levels as high as the tenth-grade level. Assuring that there is an appropriate match between the reading performance level of the learner with the readability of the printed material is necessary if appropriate growth in comprehension skill development is to take place.

9. **All elementary students should be encouraged to develop their metacognition skills in order to enhance their overall level of comprehension skill development.** Deriving meaning from various words, phrases, and sentences requires the use of many different strategies. A reader may look for certain clues to a word's meaning by examining the contextual setting of the word. In some cases the use of a dictionary may be necessary to secure the desired meaning. In yet other instances repeated rereadings with the use of certain grammar rules may be required.

Comparing the meaning of a certain passage or selection with other sources to clarify concepts and basic principles may be appropriate and useful. A known problem of understanding the affected material may be present, and thus the learner is forced to assess the reading and act upon his or her judgments to arrive at a reasonable level of understanding. All of these actions constitute the process of metacognition.[4]

10. **A child's proficiency level with regard to thinking skills is a significant correlate with his/her overall level of comprehension.** Thinking skills play an important role in reading because comprehension is largely a matter of reasoning about the text one will read, has read, or is reading. Thinking involves a large number of processes including predicting, inferring, classifying, analyzing, comparing, contrasting, cause and effect, and sequencing. These thinking skills are interdependent; for example, prediction depends on readers' ability to infer.[5]

When printed materials are placed in front of readers they are obliged to set a purpose for reading and concentrate on what concepts, facts, and ideas that are presented. Information previously obtained from various sources must be compared and contrasted with the current data and commentary being read. Learners must develop a thinking set that allows them to order and classify the various ideas and facts that are presented. They must engage in the reading act with the expectation that there is a logical body of knowledge in the text, and that meaning can finally be obtained if appropriate thinking skills are applied.

Higher order thinking processes that involve problem solving, critical thinking (fact and opinion, propaganda devices, etc.), decision making, and general creative thinking are vital to any reader for gaining increasing levels of comprehension proficiency. Posing questions on the part of all elementary teachers in both the critical and creative realms will help young children immeasurably in their quest to improve higher order thinking skills.

## FACTORS THAT INFLUENCE COMPREHENSION ABILITY

Unfortunately, a significant number of elementary students are able to pronounce words, phrases, and sentences, but they fail to demonstrate their proficiency in recalling such aspects as details, main ideas, and conclusions. Research study data appear to suggest that there is no one *single* cause for reading comprehension difficulty. (Some writers of sensational journal and newspaper articles tend to imply that the reason for the high rate of reading failure is "lack of phonics" or "poor teaching.") Those students who demonstrate low levels of comprehension ability need to be evaluated carefully through the use of informal and formal tests to help enumerate those skills areas that need further reinforcement and remediation. The most important instruments to use for this purpose include standardized achievement tests (e.g., *Iowa Test of Basic Skills, California Achievement Test*), cloze tests, informal reading inventories, and individual commercial reading tests (e.g., *Durrell Analysis of Reading Difficulty, Diagnostic Reading Scales*). Additional data may be derived by analyzing carefully the responses given by pupils to oral comprehension questions asked by the teacher.

A brief discussion of at least seven of the major factors that appear to be causal for inefficient comprehension skills development is included in this section.

1. **Certain physical problems may interfere with metacognitive and higher thinking skill performance.** Today's elementary and senior high students are functioning in an environment that has potential for many physical problems related to such aspects as drug and alcohol abuse, teenage pregnancy, eating disorders, child abuse, and overall depression. Mary Futrell, President of the National Educational Association, recently stated that "We're in the business of teaching, and we can't teach those students who are suffering from anorexia nervosa or traumatized by physical abuse, or drinking themselves into oblivion. We cannot hide from the fact that drug abuse, pregnancy, depression, anxiety, and suicide are part of our students' world." The N.E.A. provided some sobering statistics such as the following:

—about one-fourth of all high school students smoke marijuana, and more than two-thirds use alcohol.
—forty percent of today's 14-year-old girls will get pregnant in their teens.
—one of three girls and one in eight boys have reported incidents of sexual abuse.
—some 15 percent of young girls will suffer eating disorder anorexia nervosa during part or all of their teenage years.[6]

Nearly all of these conditions had their beginning when these students were at the elementary school level. Young children with serious comprehension problems should be checked carefully for any type of physical disorder that may be present.

2. **Effective comprehension requires the learner to concentrate on the**

**reading task presented.** Wilson and Cleland[7] stress this important aspect of the reading process. It is not conducive for effective comprehension to take place if boredom, difficult material, incorrect student expectations, and distractions take students off task. Many persons remember reading a page only to realize they have failed to absorb the content. Elementary teachers should be sensitive to signs that a student's mind is wandering.

In many instances a lack of concentration can be traced in large measure to a personal traumatic episode a pupil may be experiencing such as the death or divorce of a parent or physical or sexual abuse being administered. Students who appear to have maximum mental capabilities but demonstrate ineffective comprehensive skills should be analyzed carefully with regard to any of the conditions mentioned previously. Estimates of the significance of emotional factors in the causation of reading disabilities vary widely. Most students with reading difficulties show signs of emotional maladjustment which may be mild or severe. The percentage of maladjustment reported by a particular investigator varies with the standards used, as well as the student population studied.[8]

**3. One of the major causes of ineffective comprehension is a basic lack of purpose for a given reading assignment.** Either the teacher or the student must establish a purpose for reading *before* the reading process begins. For the elementary student, the teacher will no doubt be the major source of direction for the questions to be used. Merely saying "read the story and we will discuss it" leaves little if any direction for the reader regarding what *exact* kinds of information are to be remembered. In the content subjects a given assignment may include numerous facts, figures, and difficult concepts and contain dozens of subheadings with a myriad of topics presented. A situation of this nature presents a genuine dilemma for the learner because he or she is not sure if he or she is to read to remember specific details, certain main ideas, or a single generalization. When a reading assignment is given, precise questions or purposes should be given that involves all four levels of comprehension: literal, interpretive, critical, and creative. The reader's success in remembering and classifying appropriate data for these questions can be assessed through the use of commercial tests as well as teacher constructed tests and oral questions.

**4. Inappropriate background of experience is one of the important causes of poor comprehension.** Reading is much more than the simple act of pronouncing words. For each word encountered, there must be some degree of meaning generated if proper comprehension is to be obtained.

Whether students can read a passage or not depends first on their prior knowledge—on whether they have a schematic structure for the topic being discussed. In other words, an individual's reading level in a particular text depends on the topic being discussed. A topic from a typical third-grade book may be easy for one student because of familiarity with that topic, while another student in the same class may find it quite difficult due to lack of experience on the topic.[9]

If there is sufficient data to suggest that a given learner lacks sufficient understanding, the teacher has the responsibility for undertaking a variety of strategies to help build a higher level of background experience for the affected pupil. Various teaching activities may include the use of films, bulletin boards, experiments, and computer-assisted lessons from software that has been selected carefully. Directed discussions utilizing models, charts, maps, and pictures may be useful strategies for improved levels of understanding. A pretest may be given at the beginning of a unit of study to determine the exact nature of a teaching program that may be needed for individual students.

5. **Poor comprehension ability may result because the learner lacks the fundamental ability to pronounce words.** Comprehension, the *end* product of the reading act, requires the application of many skills that have been learned previously. Rapid word recognition and the knowledge of a large store of vocabulary will enable students to read quickly and with excellent understanding. Those elementary students who appear to be quite deficient in comprehension skill development should be evaluated by formal and informal evaluative measures to determine the degree and level of word attack proficiency. Listening carefully to students as they read orally may provide valuable data relating to a given learner's skill development in the areas of phonics, structural analysis, and ability to utilize context clues.

6. **There appears to be sufficient data from various research studies to suggest that inadequate comprehension ability may be the result of a low level of general intelligence.** For some elementary students the ability to comprehend different print matter of both literal and critical types is somewhat restricted because of a limited level of overall intelligence. One authority is of the belief that the relationship between intelligence test scores remains the highest obtained between any single human characteristic and reading performance. The IQ, as an index of relative level of brightness, merits serious consideration in the analysis of reading success. Reading and intelligence are positively correlates of human behavior.[10]

Intelligence test data may be used to gain a general estimate of a given child's reading expectancy age. Two of the most respected formalae include those by Albert J. Harris and Guy Bond with Miles Tinker. Harris' formula[11] is as follows:

$$Reading\ Expectancy\ Age = \frac{2(M.A.) + C.A.}{3}$$

In some ways the Bond and Tinker formula is somewhat related. The authors take into account the number of years the learner has been in a formal school setting as a part of determining reading expectancy. The teacher can compare the reading expectancy score with the data from reading achievement tests and gain appropriate knowledge regarding the level of reading potential that is being reached. The Bond and Tinker formula[12] is as follows:

$$Reading\ Expectancy = I.Q./100 \times yrs.\ of\ reading\ instruction) + 1.0$$

When using this formula, the elementary reading teacher should keep in mind several basic considerations. *First,* a high priority of importance is placed on the aspect of the intelligence quotient. Since professionals have yet to devise a completely accurate means of finding the *true* level of intelligence, any I.Q. score must be kept in proper perspective.

*Second,* kindergarten does not count in this formula. In calculating the number of years of reading instruction, one must always remember to add the number of years a grade was repeated or skipped. *Third,* the reading expectancy score is only a very general estimate of what a pupil may demonstrate with regard to reading performance. The number of variables that must be controlled makes it prohibitive to attach definite answers to such calculations.

7. **The home environment in which a pupil lives may have a significant effect on how well he/she is able to comprehend many kinds of print material.** Tragically, many students today live under the specter of child abuse and neglect. An estimated 3 percent of school age children are at risk of serious physical injury from their parents each year. Add to that number the many other children who suffer each year from physical neglect and emotional mistreatment and the number of children affected is staggering.[13]

In other situations there are problems of divorce, separation, homelessness, and unemployment. The stress associated with these conditions creates a mental structure that is counterproductive to concentration while reading, and in the final end all levels of comprehension tend to suffer. The program of diagnosis developed for those elementary children with comprehension deficiencies must always include a thorough study of the home conditions as much as possible. This may be achieved through information gained from parent-teacher conferences, reports from school psychologists, and community counselors. While many elementary teachers are not in a position to materially change the home environment, they can better plan a program of reading remediation if they have a clear understanding of the factors and forces in a child's environment that create unsatisfactory settings for learning.

If school and community policies permit, a visit to the home of a given child may provide significant, first-hand data that will help the teacher to understand the nature and conditions present in the home. Anecdotal records of such visits may be one of the significant pieces of data that are studied when causal factors are sought.

## THE COMPREHENSION SKILL LEVELS

Comprehension skills are myriad in number and complexity with some at the basic literal level with undeniable objective answers while others are critical and creative in nature and subjective, personal responses of varying types may be appropriate responses. Too many elementary teachers are content to ask oral and written questions that relate only with a large number of minute facts and figures which constitute literal data. All instructors need to challenge students with all levels of questions involving thinking critically, understanding cause and effect, and contemplating responses that are far beyond the simple "yes" or "no" to a given true-false statement, for example.

In recent years, many reading educators have attempted to place all comprehension competencies into four distinct levels: literal, interpretive, critical, and creative. A description of each of these follows.

**Literal Comprehension.** This is the lowest level of understanding and may be divided into two divisions: reproduction, which merely requires that the reader repeat the writer's words while responding to a question, while translation, the higher level of literal comprehension, requires the reader to translate or paraphrase the printed information. Neither level demands much actual thinking or analysis on the part of the reader.[14]

Many elementary students have the mistaken notion that every sentence is important in a textbook and feel that all information must be learned in a literal manner. The learner is driven to utter distraction since they find they cannot discriminate between the more important and less valuable facts and concepts that are printed. If this situation is discovered by the content teacher, he or she should provide directed instruction relative to the four levels of comprehension. He or she should emphasize that while the remembering of literal facts is important, skill must be gained in dealing with data representing the other three levels as well.

**Interpretive Comprehension.** Knowing what the author says is necessary but not sufficient in constructing meaning from print. Good readers search for conceptual complexity in material. They are capable of "reading between the lines" and focus not only on what the authors say but also on what the authors mean by what they say.[15] The interpretive or inference level consists of a number of skill components such as the following:

    a. **Selecting** the single main idea of a body of information such as a paragraph or chapter.

    b. **Discovering** the sequence of events that are described in a story, play or informative chapter and may be found in a history text.

    c. **Drawing** conclusions that are logical products of a descriptive or informative article that may be found in a science, social studies, or literature text.

    d. **Inferring** cause-and-effect relationships when those relationships and correlations are not directly stated.

    e. **Predicting** outcomes of both fictional and informational types of materials.

    f. **Generating** comparisons of such aspects as likenesses and differences in characters, times, and places.

    g. **Understanding** the precise meaning of various kinds of figurative language such as similies and metaphors.

**Critical Comprehension.** At this level elementary readers are to be actively involved in determining the truthfulness or authenticity of a statement based on their background of experience and ability to make relevant judgments about the information contained in the articles and books that are required reading. At this stage they should develop a discerning attitude that not all statements in a newspaper or book are necessarily true. Accordingly, they should develop skill in making educated judgments about whether:

a. A statement is a fact or an opinion.
b. A story is reality or fantasy.
c. The writer uses one or more propaganda techniques to promote certain ideas.
d. The material has any basic worth when compared with other articles on the same subject.
e. The text material has accuracy and truthfulness in terms of some criteria which the reader has formulated based on his/her previous experience.

One of the most important critical reading skills is that of the identification of various commonly used propaganda techniques. Readers should be given appropriate instruction to allow them to identify examples of such techniques as:

**Name-calling.** (He is a self-centered conservative on most political matters.)
**Glittering generalities.** (Everuse shoes are the standard for the discriminating buyer.)
**Plain-folks device.** (Your good neighbor, Mr. Brown, plans to vote for John Hopewell for governor.)
**Testimonials.** Eight out of ten teachers, according to a recent survery, prefer Everdry chalk to other brands.)
**Identification with prestige.** (Troy Proger, king of all cowboys, uses Jones Underslung Saddles on all of his horses.)
**Bandwagon effect.** (The Wilson poll shows that 82 percent of all registered voters prefer William Jensen for mayor.)
**Card-stacking.** (Based on the number of actual hours taught, teachers compose one of the highest paid professions now in existence.)[16]

**Creative Comprehension.** At the most advanced level of comprehension, the teacher attempts to involve the learner in the body of data presented. As opposed to fairly objective single answers for literal and interpretive questions, any logical, subjective response to creative questions must be accepted without penalty.

For example, a group of fifth-grade students has just read a long chapter in their social studies book entitled "People Move West." The materials tell about people moving from the New England states to California around 1850. The following may be appropriate creative questions:

1. Would *you* have been frightened to travel in one of the covered wagons?
2. What kind of food do you think was eaten by the pioneers?
3. What would you have done if your wagon was attacked by native Americans?

When asking questions either orally or written, it is important to be sure to include items at *all* four levels of comprehension. In some instances, use the questions as guiding purposes for each silent reading assignment. At the conclusion of the silent reading, use recitation techniques to see if the pupils found the answers to the questions.

## TEACHING PROCEDURES FOR BUILDING EFFECTIVE UNDERSTANDING

There are many strategies that may be utilized for building comprehension skill proficiencies at all four comprehension levels that were discussed in the previous section. The following are a sampling of ideas that may be used with elementary students.[17]

**Literal Comprehension**

1. Read three or four paragraphs from the class text or other material. Ask the students to write as many separate details as they can remember from the oral reading. They should not be permitted to take notes during the reading of the paragraphs.
2. Provide a printed copy of an outline of a chapter or unit of material. List a number of details which are included in the selection. The students should be asked to check the detail which is associated with a particular aspect of the outline.
3. Supply each student with a six-paragraph length selection from a class text. At the end of the paragraphs, list ten sentences. If the sentence consists of a detail which was included in the selection, the letter "Y" (yes) should be placed before the sentence. If the statement does not contain a significant detail, the letter "N" (no) should be placed on the blank.
4. Write announcements or directions for a class project on the chalkboard, overhead projector, or on a piece of paper. State that oral directions will not be given. Students should understand that they need to read and follow directions and become independent

in this regard. Some persons have developed poor listening habits since they expect the teacher to repeat oral directions several times. Written directions without further explanation help to eliminate this unfortunate habit.

5. Ask students to engage in an exercise which is designed to emphasize the importance of following directions. At the top of a lesson sheet print the following statement: **"You are to read all directions for the exercise before beginning the lesson."** The second statement might read, "Write your middle name on the blank." The third direction might be "Write yes or no if you think you are a good reader." Continue the exercise with various directions of this type. The last statement should read, "Follow none of the previous directions. Hand in your blank paper to your teacher immediately." The results are dramatic and obvious to many students.

## Interpretive Comprehension

1. Demonstrate the meaning and importance of subtopics found in a chapter. Show how the subtopic titles compose the main idea of the material which follows. Duplicate two or three pages of materials from a text with the subtopics deleted during the duplicating process. Ask the students to read the paragraphs and supply a subtopic which would constitute the main idea of the printed material.

2. Provide students with copies of a three- or four-paragraph selection of printed material utilized in class. Supply four sentences at the end of the material. One of the four sentences constitutes the main idea of the paragraphs. The other three sentences have little relationship to the subject. Ask students to select the main idea. Demonstrate why a given statement is the main idea.

3. After discussing the features of a duplicated map of Europe, ask the students to respond to questions such as these:
   a. What countries border the country of France?
      _____
   b. Write the name of a range of mountains found in Europe.
      _____
   c. What symbol is used to designate the capital cities of the various countries?_____
   d. Name the largest city in the country of Holland.
      _____

   e. The shortest distance across the English Channel is
      approximately _____ miles.
4. Ask the students to read a certain section of a chapter in the class
   textbook. The material should be two to four pages in length and
   cover one major topic as a part of the total chapter. Emphasize to
   them the importance of examining summary and topic sentences
   which may be included. Provide four different short summaries
   which have been duplicated on four different pieces of paper. Ask
   students to select the most suitable summary for the material.
   They should provide an explanation of why they think their
   chosen summary is better than the other three. The teacher should
   reveal his or her choice and why that particular summary is more
   applicable than the rest.

**Critical Comprehension**

1. To give students practice in differentiating between fact and opinion,
   ask them to place the letter "F" before all statements which they
   believe are facts and the letter "O" before all statements which are
   merely opinions. The following may be examples used for a
   geography class.
   a. Denver is the capital city of Colorado.
   b. The best winter climate is found in the state of Florida.
   c. The richest farmland is found on the banks of the Mississippi
      River.
   d. The state with the largest land area in the continental United
      States is Texas.
   e. More wheat is raised in Kansas than in Georgia
   f. Pikes Peak is the most beautiful of all mountains in the United
      States.
2. Discuss the following propaganda techniques and examples with
   class members:
      a. **Name calling**—radical, conservative, right-wing
      b. **Sweeping generalizations**—the answer to your dreams,
         the standard of quality.
      c. **Bandwagon**—everyone in this neighborhood has bought
         an excel broom.
      d. **Identification with prestige**—Elvet Hudson, movie star,
         has bought two Conokot automobiles.

e. **Card-stacking**—only 3 percent of the population can be considered poor or destitute.

## Creative Comprehension

1. Show students various pictures of exciting events such as a football player crossing the goal line or a car sliding down a steep ditch. Ask "how would you have felt in these situations?"
2. Ask pupils to read several short selections about various famous people. Ask each one to tell why he/she thinks each person is famous.
3. Read short stories to the pupils involving characters in dangerous places. Ask them what they would do in each instance.

## SUMMARY

Comprehension is the end product of the reading act. Teachers must understand that there are many facts to comprehension and that the total process consists of four levels.

Many students fail to comprehend because of negative factors such as physical, emotional, and intellectual aspects. A careful diagnosis must be undertaken to determine what strategies to undertake to remediate certain deficiencies.

The strategies mentioned at the close of the chapter should prove helpful for both developmental and remedial teaching. All pupils need to be helped to reach their maximum potential with regard to comprehension skills proficiencies.

## REFERENCES

1. Gray, Mary Jane, "Comprehension Process or Product?" *Reading Horizons*, V. 27, N. 2, (Winter, 1986) p. 146.
2. Clary, Linda M., "Twelve Musts For Improved Reading Comprehension," *Reading Horizons*, V. 26, N. 2 (Winter, 1986), pp. 99–100.
3. Clary, p. 102.
4. Karlin, Robert and Andrea R. Karlin, *Teaching Elementary Reading Principles and Strategies* (Fourth Edition). New York, Harcourt Brace Jovanovich, 1987, p. 244.
5. Stoodt, Barbara D. *Reading Instruction* (Second Edition). New York, Harper & Row, 1989, p. 179.

6. _____ "Students' Problems Reach Crisis Levels," *Omaha World-Herald,* August 15, 1986, p. 10.

7. Wilson, Robert M. and Craig J. Cleland. *Diagnostic and Remedial Reading for Classroom and Clinic* (Sixth Edition). Columbus, Merrill, 1989, p. 269.

8. Harris, Albert J. and Edward R. Sipay. *How to Increase Reading Ability* (Seventh Edition). New York, Longman, 1980, p. 316.

9. Duffy, Gerald G. and Laura R. Roehler. *Improving Classroom Reading Instruction: A Decision-Making Approach* (Second Edition). New York, Random House, 1989, p. 190.

10. Hill, Walter R. *Secondary School Reading: Process, Program, Procedure.* Boston, Allyn and Bacon, 1979, p. 31.

11. Harris, Albert J. and Edward R. Sipay. *How To Increase Reading Ability* (Eighth Edition). New York, Longman, 1985, p. 152.

12. Bond, Guy L., Miles A. Tinker, Barbara B. Wasson, and John B. Wasson. *Reading Difficulties, Their Diagnosis and Correction* (Fifth Edition). Englewood Cliffs, Prentice-Hall, 1984, pp. 42–45.

13. Wilson and Cleland, pp. 91–92.

14. Miller, Wilma. *The First R Elementary Reading Today* (Second Edition). Prospect Heights, Illinois, Waveland Press, 1983, p. 196.

15. Vacca, Richard T. and JoAnne L. Vacca. *Content Area Reading* (Second Edition). Boston, Little, Brown, 1986, p. 147.

16. Cushenbery, Donald C. *Comprehensive Reading Strategies For All Secondary Students.* Springfield, Charles C Thomas, 1988, pp. 75–77.

17. Cushenbery, Donald C. *Improving Reading Skills In The Content Areas.* Springfield, Charles C Thomas, 1985, pp. 64–71.

Chapter VI

# READING SKILLS IN THE CONTENT AREAS

Teaching reading skills is not an activity that takes place only during the "reading" period. All teachers need to keep in mind that reading is a process that permeates the entire curriculum. Reading skills such as those in the areas of word attack, comprehension, and vocabulary should be promoted in such content areas as social studies, science, and health.

The criticism is frequently made that pupils perform very well as readers in the primary grades but encounter difficulties when they examine the textbooks and expository materials found in the middle grades. Although content textbooks are used previous to fourth grade, the writing styles used in them changes in the middle grade. Many middle-grade teachers expect students to read text and learn independently. In general, middle-grade teachers expect pupils to learn *how* to read in the primary grades; therefore, they expect these learners to use their reading skills to acquire new knowledge.[1] There are a number of other problems involved in reading content material. Durkin[2] notes that subject-matter textbooks are not made up of consistently well written, interesting prose. Actually, some content is so irrelevant for elementary school students as to require asking why an author ever decided to include it. Some of the students who are expected to acquire information from these textbooks do not even come close to having the reading ability or the experiences that the expectation assumes.

The elementary teacher must assume a direct strategic role in planning and directing reading skill lessons in every content lesson. To provide appropriate information that is both germane and practical, the following topics are discussed in this chapter: skills involved in content reading; approaches for content reading skill development; and evaluating content reading competency.

## SKILLS INVOLVED IN CONTENT READING

Though the skills involved in everyday developmental reading and content reading are somewhat similar, several of them are distinctly unique if a reader is to have success in reading content materials. There are a number of inherent difficulties that are common to content materials that must be recognized. Accordingly each learner must be able to build the following skill components.

1. **Recognize that all content materials contain technical vocabulary and each subject or content area utilizes certain words and phrases not common to stories, plays, and poems found in most basal readers.** Some examples of such words are as follows:

> Social Studies: *canal, culture, parallel, longitude, latitude, monetary.*
> Science: *propel, rotation, centrificial, protons, calculate, electrons, eclipse.*
> Mathematics: *numerators, obtuse, multiples, dividend, product, fraction.*
> Health: *ancestors, vitamins, deficiencies, supplements, dietary, contagious.*

2. **Understand the principle that the writing style encountered in content reading is usually considerably different from that found in stories in most basal reader books.** The sentences are usually shorter and contain several important words in a single, short sentence. One must read every word and engage in intense concentration in order to understand all of the concepts. There is no freedom to skip certain sentences or paragraphs. In social studies, a few short paragraphs may cover 50 years of time. An important experiment may be dealt with in three succinct paragraphs.

3. **Note that the structure of the writing found in many content texts makes for a high readability level because of the complex concepts presented, various grammars outlined, and the massive amount of technical vocabulary inculcated in the explanatory text.** In many instances, a significant amount of data is presented in the context of critical and creative comprehension modes that demand the reader be competent with all of the higher level thinking and understanding skills. The graphic aids carry an inordinate amount of significant facts and figures that may seem overwhelming to the young reader.

4. **Constructs the undeniable thought structure that a high level of proficiency in everyday study skills is both urgent and necessary if suitable**

**levels of comprehension and vocabulary competency is to be obtained when dealing with content area reading.** The elementary reading teacher may wish to use the following evaluation sheet for taking an honest assessment of the current level of ability of *each* pupil in this important area.

## Evaluation of Study Skills*

Name _____  School _____
Grade _____  Date _____

|  |  | Satisfactory | Unsatisfactory |
|---|---|---|---|
| 1. | Completes school assignments by following directions accurately. | _____ | _____ |
| 2. | Exhibits ability to summarize various pieces of content reading material while retaining important information segments | _____ | _____ |
| 3. | Notes topic sentences and understands their usefulness in securing the main idea of a section or chapter. | _____ | _____ |
| 4. | Senses the purpose and appropriate rate of reading which should be employed in reading a particular selection. | _____ | _____ |
| 5. | Selects important details and remembers those which may be needed for examinations or class discussions. | _____ | _____ |
| 6. | Demonstrates skill in finding the author's purpose for writing a particular piece of printed matter. | _____ | _____ |
| 7. | Detects the sequence of events which are outlined in a given content selection. | _____ | _____ |
| 8. | Selects important information from various graphic aids found in science and mathematics texts. | _____ | _____ |
| 9. | Knows how to interpret the information depicted on such textbook items as maps, graphs, and charts. | _____ | _____ |
| 10. | Notes appropriate resources such as the *World Almanac* for assignments which require detailed information. | _____ | _____ |

*From Donald C. Cushenbery, *Improving Reading Skills in the Content Area,* 1985, pp. 73–75. Courtesy of Charles C Thomas, Publisher, Springfield, Illinois.

11. Follows oral directions given by the
    teacher regarding such aspects as
    assignments and projects. _____ _____
12. Determines which words and/or phrases
    should be underlined when constructing
    class notes. _____ _____
13. Demonstrates skill in skimming and
    scanning long selections for the purpose
    of selecting main ideas. _____ _____
14. Knows how to utilize the various class-
    room encyclopedias as sources for
    desired data. _____ _____
15. Exhibits an understanding of the use and
    importance of the table of contents,
    index, and glossary of a content book. _____ _____
16. Understands and uses various appendices
    of content and resource books. _____ _____

5. **Demonstrates** that he/she has a thorough understanding of several basic principles with regard to structural analysis. Breaking words apart and spelling them correctly are important for understanding words, phrases, and sentences in any content lesson. The following principles should be taught and reviewed with all elementary children as they engage in content reading.

a) If a root word ends with the letter "e," the "e" is dropped when an ending that begins with a vowel is added: (take, taking).

b) If a syllable or word ends in a single consonant preceded by a vowel, the consonant is often doubled when an ending is added: (map, mapped; net, netted).

c) Numerous words can be formed by merely adding an inflectional ending with no change in the root word (picked, girls, masking, watches).

d) In situations where a word ends with the letter "y" preceded by a consonant, the "y" is normally changed to an "i" before an ending is added: (manliness, fatalities). If the "y" is preceded by a vowel, there is usually no change in the root word when an ending is added: (ploys, bays).

e) Words that end in "f" or "fe" often form their plurals by changing the "f" to a "v" and adding the plural endings: (knives, scarves).

Due to the fact that there is much attention given to syllabication as a part of an overall program of structural analysis instruction, several basic principles should be reviewed and understood by all elementary students.

a) Every syllable encountered in any recognizable common or proper word must contain either a vowel or vowel sound: (in, Srb).

b) If a word contains a prefix and root word, the word is usually divided between the two meaning units: (unable, mistake).

c) When two consonants are preceded and followed by a vowel, the word is normally divided into syllables after the first vowel that is usually long: (be-hind, mi-ler, mo-tel).

d) If a word ends in a consonant with the letters "le" at the end, the word is divided before the consonant: (ma-ple, pur-ple, ap-ple).

e) When two consonants are surrounded by two vowels, the word is normally separated into syllables between the two consonants with the first vowel retaining a short sound (of-ten, mop-per).

6. **Analyzes words in a sentence pattern in order to arrive at the approximate meaning that should be applied to them.** In many instances, the words in the body of the context will not provide a meaning clue; thus, the reader is forced to depend on the dictionary as a final source of information.

Generally speaking, all types of context clues can be grouped into two major divisions: syntactical or structural tools and format or typographical strategies. The former group involves the use of synonyms, antonyms, and appositives and various cause-effect relationships. The latter facet deals with various textbook features such as the glossary, reference sections, underlined and italicized words and phrases, and footnotes of various kinds.

There are eight types or kinds of context clues that are generally found in most reading material. They are as follows:

a) **Summary.** (The unknown word or phrase outlines the ideas that precede it.) *Example:* The several houses that were destroyed in the tornado represented a major **calamity** for the owners involved.

b) **Association.** (The unfamiliar word is associated or related to a known word.) *Example:* He ran the race and won easily with the **preciseness** of a true champion.

c) **Contrast.** (The unknown word has a meaning opposite of the known word.) *Example:* He was the father of the tribe while she was the **matriarch.**

d) **Precise Description.** (The unfamiliar word is defined directly in the sentence.) *Example:* The ugly, frightful animal was indeed a very **hideous** creature.

e) **Mood Reflection.** (The unknown words correlate with a mood or feeling which has been built into the sentence.) *Example:* The disrespectful people in the church service gave us the idea that they were very **irreverent.**

f) **Restatement.** (The unfamiliar word is explained in the statement.) *Example:* The **omniscient** person appeared to have complete and infinite knowledge about the entire field of chemistry.

g) **Experience Background.** (The unknown word's meaning can be derived by using the reader's background of experience.) *Example:* At the dance several **minuets** were played for those who wanted to dance slowly and stately.

h) **Inference.** (The meaning of the word can be derived in light of the reader's familiarity with everyday expressions.) *Example:* When I was in the hospital, the nurse had me swallow different kinds of medications.[3]

7. **Demonstrates the ability to use a classroom dictionary in the proper manner in order to find the best meaning for a given word that is being studied.** Hopefully each pupil will have a copy of a dictionary that is designed for his/her reading and interest levels. The glossaries found in many textbooks may also prove to be useful. Lessons should be provided for students that will give them both developmental and remedial practice in building important dictionary skills.

The following is a sample exercise that may be constructed for use with elementary students.

*Directions:* You have been provided with a class dictionary. Below are five statements with underlined words. Following the sentences are three pairs of guide words from three pages in the dictionary. Write the number of the page where the underlined word would be found.

1. **The *hickory* is a North American tree in the same family as the walnut. (a) *Page 283,* hibernate-highland; (b) *Page 284,* highlander-hinder; (c) *Page 285,* hindermost-history.**

2. That old man is very *eccentric.* (a) *Page 120,* **earache-easily;** (b) *Page 121,* **easiness-eatable;** (c) *Page 122,* **eaten-echidna.**

3. **The cowboy used a** *goad* **for driving the cattle to the pasture.** (a) *Page 134,* **gnomic-goat;** (b) *Page 135,* **goatee-golden;** (c) *Page 136,* **goldfish-goodish.**

4. **The piano player gave a** *masterful* **performance during the entire concert.** (a) *Page 389,* **marquise-martyr;** (b) *Page 390,* **martyrdom-massive;** (c) **massy-mastic.**

5. **He** *forbid* **me from going to the circus.** (a) *Page 149,* **folio-football;** (b) *Page 150,* **footgear-forage;** (c) *Page 151,* **foray-foreclose.**[4]

**8. Gives evidence that he/she can utilize surveying techniques to gain a general understanding relative to the major topic(s) being studied.** The importance of this skill is emphasized by Karlin and Karlin[5] who mention that whether pupils are required to read and obtain information from single sources or multiple ones, pupils will be helped by a broad overview of the contents of each of the books they will be using. The knowledge of how the book is organized and what special features it contains should be most important. Pupils should examine their textbooks under the teacher's direction previous to their actual reading of the source.

A careful survey of a book, for example, calls for the reader to note the titles of chapters and to glance over all of the major headings. The total process may be thought of as skimming and might include five separate steps.

a) **Read** the chapter and introductory paragraphs. Note if one of the sentences is a topic sentence.
b) **Read** and look carefully at the headings that are in bold-face.
c) **Skim** all of the pages and give close attention to all words and phrases that are italicized.
d) **Read** the captions with care and look for special features such as maps, charts, graphs, and pictures.
e) **Read** the summary provided by the author if one appears at the end of the chapter.

**9. Demonstrates the ability to use advance organizers (such as a semantic web) when they are provided by the teacher.** Pupils can gain very valuable information from a body of print matter when they organize significant facts, and concepts from such techniques as brief summaries, skeleton outlines, and a structured overview or semantic web. The following is a semantic web that was constructed from the data presented regarding a chapter in the elementary science book relating to plant and animal life.

**Plant and Animal Life**

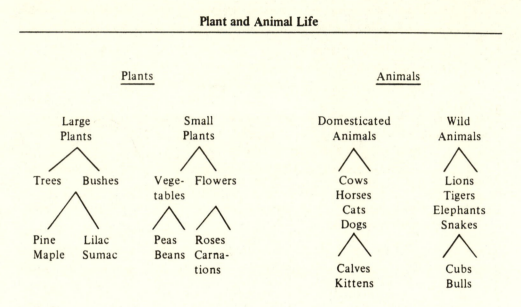

10. Shows proficiency in using various rates of reading speed when understanding silent reading assignments involving both content books and resource volumes. There are four general types or rates of reading that can be employed by learners. They are **detailed reading** (up to 135 words per minute; **average rate** (135 to 400 words per minute); **skimming** (400 to 2,000 words per minutes); and **scanning** (*over* 2,000 words per minute). The following are some classroom situations that would be appropriate for use with the four speeds.

  I. **Detailed Reading**
    a. **The name of the first President of the United States was**

        _____.

    b. **Name three countries that are located in South America.**

        _____　_____　_____

    c. **America sent the first man into space orbit on** _____.
 II. **Average Rate**
    a. **What is the main idea of the third paragraph?**

    b. What two major chemicals are discussed on page 4?

    c. Name three types of weather discussed on pages 5 and 6.

III. Skimming

    a. Skim the table of contents and then tell me if the author discusses prehistoric man in the book.

    b. Skim the map of South America on page 49 of the social studies book. What is the name of the highest mountain on this continent?

    c. Look at the charts on pages 86 and 87. What are the names of the three chief coal mining areas of the United States?

IV. Scanning

    a. Open to page 123 of your text. Find the names of the last four presidents of the United States.

    b. Notice the map of Canada on page 142. Write the names of four cities with populations of 50,000 or more.

    c. Look at the two graphs on page 162. What are the leading exports of Ecuador, Brazil, and Mexico?

## APPROACHES FOR CONTENT
## READING SKILLS DEVELOPMENT

There are many strategies available to elementary teachers for helping pupils improve reading skills in all of the content areas. Certainly one of the major suggestions would be to read carefully all of the many teaching suggestions that may be a part of the teacher's edition for each content book. Many authors supply important recommendations regarding such items as reading objectives, vocabulary, and comprehension development. Recommendations for further reading may also be included.

Several important strategy strands can be especially helpful to elementary teachers in improving overall reading skill development in the content areas. They are (1) the five-step approach for teaching reading skills in the content area; (2) study skills procedures; and (3) the cloze technique for analysis and teaching of reading skills. These are described in the section that follows.

## I. Five-Step Approach to Teaching Reading in the Content Areas

**The five-step approach to teaching reading in the content areas should be followed during every class session when print media is used.** This approach helps to provide a background of readiness for reading, establish a purpose for reading, and build important reading skills. The five stages are as follows:

### a. Readiness Stage

At the beginning of the lesson, the teacher asks the students to survey the chapter or reading section to secure an idea about the major topics presented and to get an overall impression regarding the general facts and concepts which are presented. Careful attention should be given to the names of the major and minor headings. The teacher may wish to ask the students if they have any background or data relating to these topics. Some time should be spent by the teacher in "selling" the importance of the topics to the students. Mention should be made of why this topic is relevant to the total content subject which is being studied. Building appropriate readiness for a topic may well be the **most important key** to total comprehension.

### b. Question or Purpose Stage

Since one of the leading causes of ineffective comprehension is lack of purpose for reading, it is important for questions or purposes to be established for the pending reading assignment. The number of questions formed should depend on the age and attention span of the learners. For example, a four-page assignment for fourth graders may involve only three or four major questions, while a seven-page section for sixth grade students may include the use of six or seven questions. The questions assigned should be from all four of the comprehension levels: **literal, interpretive, critical,** and **creative.** For example, if a social studies class is studying "The Westward Movement," the teacher may wish to pose the following questions or purposes for reading:

**Literal:** What was the name given to the covered wagons which carried freight across the prairie?
**Interpretive:** From looking at the subtopics on Pages 60–62, what do you think is the main idea of this material?
**Critical:** After reading Section Three on Pages 68–74, indicate if the

following statement is a fact or an opinion. **The major reason for the westward movement was to search for gold.**

**Creative:** If you had been living in 1845 in the New England area, would you have joined the westward movement? Why or why not?

### c. Silent Reading Stage

After having posed the questions, the students should then read silently in books and other print media which are at their **instructional reading levels.** If the silent reading takes place during the class period, the teacher should observe the reading habits of students with particular attention given to such aspects as head movements and finger pointing. Students who appear to be frustrated by the assignment may need special remedial help from a reading specialist. Those who find the material too difficult to read may need reading assignments which are at a lower level of difficulty.

### d. Discussion Stage

When the silent reading of the text has been completed, an oral discussion should take place. The questions or purposes which were formulated in the second stage should be utilized for this purpose. Those students who have difficulty in finding the answers should be directed to use specific study or reading skill improvement techniques which may be recommended by the content teacher.

### e. Culminating Activity Stage

Some type of class activity such as a bulletin board, a time-line, or summary paper should be constructed which will serve to bring together the major topics which have been presented in the previous chapters or sections. In other words, better comprehension of the material results when the students can see the relationship(s) which exists among and between the various discussion topics.[6]

## II. Study Skills Procedures

Duffy and Roehler[7] are of the belief that study strategies can be organized into five categories, all of which are used metacognitively. They are **locational strategies, rate strategies, remembering strategies, organizing strategies,** and **study habits.** A description follows of what is involved with each of these categories.

The **LOCATIONAL STRATEGIES** include all of the instructional objectives involved with helping elementary pupils locate desired information relating to a given topic that may be in the process of being studied in such subjects as social studies, health, and science. Pupils need to know how to use the card catalogs in the school media center. In the same room they need to find significant information located in encyclopedias, atlases, and other similar materials. They should receive specific instruction regarding how to use maps, graphs, and charts found in informational source books.

**RATE OF READING** strategies involving the four rates described earlier should be stressed. Carefully planned lessons that require the learner to use these rates should be undertaken.

**REMEMBERING TECHNIQUES** involve the use of reading-study formulae such as SQ3R developed by Francis Robinson. This formula provides learners with a structured step-by-step procedure for surveying material, asking questions to guide reading, undertaking silent reading, answering the guiding questions, and reviewing what has been learned.

One of the most important remembering strategies promoted by many teachers is the use of **mnemonics**. During the years that a child spends in an elementary school, he/she is expected to learn certain sequential bodies of data and information such as the alphabet, days of the week, and months of the year. Committing data to memory is an important part of the total educational process and yet many elementary teachers fail to use mnemonic techniques to help children remember. There is a considerable amount of research data to support the belief that memory can be improved considerably through visual and memory elaboration procedures. A mnemonic technique is essentially a process of transforming or altering essential to-be-learned data into a form that makes it easier to remember.

**Summarization** is an excellent memory device. The reader is taught to connect together in several sentences the essential parts of a longer passage that has been read at some previous time. The activity requires the learner to separate less important sentences and paragraphs from those that are absolutely essential for total meaning.

**ORGANIZING STRATEGIES** basically involve the use of such common procedures as taking notes and outlining the major topics noted in a body of material.[8] Through the use of semantic mapping (described earlier) the teacher can demonstrate to pupils how various ideas relate to one another. Major headings with connecting ideas and subjects help learners to grasp and organize the total structure of a topic or selection. In some cases it is best for the pupils themselves to construct the semantic map with the peer group acting as the constructive critics to arrive at a concensus regarding the body of information presented.

**STUDY HABITS** can be helped greatly through the use of some recognized study strategy such as the R.E.A.P procedure developed by Eanet and Manzo.[9] There are four basic steps to the procedure:

R—**Read** the assigned material and try to select the main idea(s) which the author(s) sought to project to the reader.

E—**Encode** the main ideas and rewrite these data into the vocabulary and thought processes of the learner.

A—**Annotate** the information to provide a meaningful summary for remembering data for a test or sharing with the teacher or fellow classmates as the occasion demands.

P—**Ponder** the material and determine the thesis of the writer's message and how it relates to the general body of information already known and understood about a topic.

## III. The Cloze Technique

One of the most useful of all classroom reading tests is the cloze technique instrument. The test is especially useful in determining a student's ability in vocabulary, word attack, and comprehension skills. The test is easily constructed from using textbook material which is utilized in everyday reading assignments. The following are the steps to use in constructing such a test.

1. Select a 260–280 word passage in the middle part of the class text or other source book.
2. On a piece of 8½″ by 11″ paper, type the first sentence as it appears in the material.
3. Beginning with the second sentence, leave every fifth or sixth word blank until a total of 50 blanks have been accumulated.
4. Ask the students to write a word on each blank which they think is the most logical.
5. Check each student's paper allowing credit for each word which is the **same** as the one in the original text. **No** credit should be given for synonyms.

For the purposes of scoring, the teacher should use the following standards.

**26–50 correct** — independent reading level. (The student is capable of reading a more difficult text.)

**18–25 correct** — instructional reading level. (The student can read this material at a satisfactory level.)

**17–0 correct** — frustration reading level. (The student **cannot** read this material in a satisfactory manner.)

Since a student's performance on the cloze test may be influenced by background of experience and other factors, the cloze test should be administered over at least three different parts of the book. As noted earlier, the decision concerning a pupil's reading ability should be based on a **pattern** of scores and not just the score from a single test.

The cloze technique can also be used as a **teaching device** rather than as a testing technique. The following are suggestions for the construction of various teaching lessons.

1. Provide the students with copies of the technique with the 50 blanks. Place the list of 50 words which came from the book in a scrambled list. Ask the pupils to select words from the list for the blanks. They should draw a line through each word as it is used.

2. Ask pupils to write a word of **their** choice on the blanks. Invite them to read aloud their selection with the words they supplied. Have them listen carefully to note the comparison of meaning emphasis displayed by each person.

3. Provide copies of the exercise and supply a multiple choice list of three words for each blank. One of the words should be the word from the original text, another word should be reasonably logical, and the third word should be an absurdity.[10]

## EVALUATING CONTENT READING COMPETENCY

There are numerous methods and procedures available to elementary teachers for evaluating the reading competency levels of their students. They may be grouped into three major categories: (a) commercial achievement tests that are norm-referenced; (b) commercial informal tests that are mostly diagnostic in nature; and (c) teacher-made individual diagnostic instruments. Each test or strategy has its unique advantages and limitations and must be carefully scrutinized by the teacher before it is used with a given child. The names and accompanying brief descriptions are included in the section that follows. (A complete discussion of the evaluation of reading skills can be found in the last chapter.)

## I. Commercial Norm-Referenced Reading Tests

There are numerous tests in this category that can be useful to the content teacher. Examples of such tests include the *California Reading Tests, Gates-MacGinitie Reading Tests, Iowa Tests of Basic Skills,* and the *Metropolitan Reading Tests.* The publishers of these and similar tests can provide computerized scoring services that include such data as percentile and stanine scores along with detailed item analysis profiles showing which pupils need precise, individualized instruction for improving certain reading skills. Class profiles can also be constructed to show which groups of learners need instruction in such areas as reading maps, graphs, and charts and general vocabulary and comprehension ability.

## II. Commercial Informal Tests

Reading specialists use numerous commercial instruments in individual situations to try to find the specific strengths and limitations of certain learners. The more widely used tests in this category include the *Durrell Analysis of Reading Difficulty, Gates-McKillop Reading Diagnostic Test, Gray Oral Reading Test, Gilmore Oral Reading Test,* and the *Woodcock Reading Mastery Tests.*

## III. Teacher-Made Individual Diagnostic Tests

A number of these kinds of tests are described in the last chapter of this volume. The cloze test (described earlier) is one of the most important tests in this category. Others that may be utilized include the **subjective reading inventory, individual sight word vocabulary inventory,** and **the incomplete sentences test.** The data derived from these strategies can be integrated with the information obtained from commercial tests to form a data base for forming appropriate developmental and remedial reading lessons for those students who have pronounced deficiencies in the major content reading areas.

## SUMMARY

There are numerous skills involved in reading content materials that are not present when reading basal materials stories. Elementary teachers must recognize that reading is **not a subject** that is taught only during a certain period of the day but rather a **process** that encompasses the total school day and relates to **all** curriculum areas.

The elementary teacher has a number of significant teaching modes or strategies that can be used to improve overall content area reading skills. These include such procedures as the five-step approach to teaching reading, the cloze techniques, and certain study procedures.

Major reading skill components can be analyzed through the use of such instruments as commercial norm-referenced tests, commercial individualized diagnostic instruments, and teacher-made tests. The results obtained from these measures can be of much help to instructors in planning and implementing appropriate content reading lessons.

## REFERENCES

1. Stoodt, Barbara D. *Reading Instruction* (Second Edition). New York, Harper & Row, 1989, p. 339.
2. Durkin, Dolores. *Teaching Them To Read* (Fifth Edition). Boston, Allyn and Bacon, 1989, p. 431.
3. Cushenbery, Donald C. *Improving Reading Skills In The Content Area.* Springfield, Charles C Thomas, 1985, pp. 42–43.
4. Cushenbery, p. 49.
5. Karlin, Robert and Andrea R. Karlin. *Teaching Elementary Reading Principles and Strategies* (Fourth Edition). New York, Harcourt Brace Jovanovich, 1987, p. 301.
6. Cushenbery, pp. 59–61.
7. Duffy, Gerald G. and Laura R. Roehler. *Improving Classroom Reading Instruction, a Decision-Making Process.* New York, Random House, 1989, pp. 148–152.
8. Duffy and Roehler, p. 151.
9. Eanet, Marilyn and Anthony V. Manzo, "REAP—A Strategy for Improving Reading/Writing/Study Skills," *Journal of Reading,* V. 19 (May, 1976), pp. 647–652.
10. Cushenbery, pp. 40–41.

Chapter VII

# MOTIVATING READING INTEREST THROUGH A LITERATURE-BASED CURRICULUM AND COOPERATIVE LEARNING

In recent years there have been numerous additional strategies applied to the traditional basal reading materials approach to make learning experiences more meaningful and useful to readers at all ability levels. Two of these important trends have been the massive amounts of literature selections that have been introduced to provide all readers with practice in reading all types of print media. The other movement has been the extended practice of cooperative learning involving children who are placed in innovative learning environments whereby it is possible for pupils to gain significant cognitive and affective knowledge from their peers.

The purpose of this major chapter is to present a body of research-based practical information that will allow the classroom teacher to create a viable classroom curriculum that embodies motivational practices that are complemented by cooperative learning activities and a literature-based reading program. To accomplish this purpose, the following topics are included in this chapter: the importance of motivation; utilizing a literature-based curriculum; and role of cooperative learning in reading instruction.

## THE IMPORTANCE OF MOTIVATION

A causal observation of the work habits of large numbers of pupils lends one to the inescapable conclusion that some pupils learn to read successfully with much joy and enthusiasm while others look upon the activity with boredom and utter disdain. Observers of the human learners have come to acknowledge a generally accepted belief that there are numerous reasons why some elementary children fail in their goal of building reading skill levels. Some educators believe that one of the significant reasons is a general lack of motivation. For many pupils a required class assigned reading lesson (with an accompanying test) is not sufficient motivation for many children to read.

One notes elementary pupils in any given classroom at any grade level and observes several who are reading with eagerness and enthusiasm while another group of learners in the same classroom appear to be lethargic and bored. The unmotivated students must be identified and appropriate strategies applied to help *all* readers achieve at their *maximum* learning levels.

Practically all pupils have a desire or wish to improve, challenge, or impress their peers and/or teacher. In the area of reading, the young child must be inspired to try new experiences that will result in additional academic enrichment for his/her life.

Obviously, one of the major means of gaining new knowledge is through reading the printed word. A student who wishes to gain a large body of new knowledge must obviously be motivated to read a variety of print media. The source for much of the elementary pupil's level of motivation must necessarily reside primarily with the classroom teacher. Too many teachers think that the threat of the administration of an achievement or teacher-made test is a sufficient reason for a learner to want to read a story in a basal reader or a selection in a content book. Unfortunately, a few pupils see no urgent purpose for reading and have the opinion that the teacher, in the final analysis, will not fail them and they will be promoted to the next grade.

Many parents of young children often wonder why their son, Billy, or daughter, Margaret, read with eagerness and enthusiasm in Miss H's third-grade class but developed a disdain for reading assignments in Miss Z's fourth-grade room. To develop a rather complete understanding of the situation, a study of several important factors must be undertaken. Several of these aspects are noted in the following section.

1. **The physical aspects of the classroom may have a detrimental effect on the motivational level of an elementary reader.** With this in mind, daily assessments should be made relative to such conditions as room temperature, noise level, and relative comfort of classroom furniture. Some studies suggest that the location of the classroom relative to the music room, physical education gymnasium, and other areas may have an effect on a pupil's level of academic achievement.

2. **An appropriate curriculum with concomitant award systems should be established to help insure success for the student.** Very few students

really want to fail. Most learners understand the penalties for failure and are motivated to succeed if there are sufficient provisions made in the course of studies for success.

3. **The curiosity level of an elementary student can be raised considerably with the right type of instruction.** Most learners possess a degree of natural curiosity to learn. They can be motivated to develop interest if they are given books they can read successfully and are within their range of interest. Much attention should be given to match teaching style with the preferred learning modes of individual students. Special attention should be given to "at-risk" students.

4. **Elementary teachers must take into account that there are strong environmental influences that affect motivation for reading.** A careful study of the total schedule of activities for some young children appears to show that many of them spend as many as 28 to 35 clock hours per week watching television. Other activities may include music lessons, soccer games, and community clubs. Some pupils have made the conscious decision that the nonschool programs have a higher priority than reading during the school day. Because of these conditions, teachers must correlate reading assignments as closely as possible with after school activities.

5. **Teachers are the most important role models that many elementary pupils may have.** Unfortunately, some children are subjected to physical and emotional abuse and may not be reared in a suitable home environment. Unfortunately, a few elementary teachers present an impression that they have little personal interest in reading. In such cases, the young child may feel that he/she does not need to develop a motivation for reading widely.

In summary, motivation is a key factor in helping to insure a maximum level of reading success for all elementary children who are pursuing a program of developmental and/or remedial reading. Unless the young pupils realize some success in performing the reading act, they will have great difficulty in understanding the importance of reading as a critical part in their lives. The careful analysis of each learner's reading interests and attitudes is vital if programs for building motivation are to succeed. Every instructor needs to be a role model for the total class and use appropriate techniques that will help insure a maximum level of success for each child.

## UTILIZING A LITERATURE-BASED CURRICULUM

Many elementary reading specialists have concluded from careful observation and the results of various research studies that any given pupil should have the benefit of reading a wide range of literature — not just the stories that happen to appear in a given basal-level reading book.

Teachers using a literature-based curriculum center their instruction on using "real" books rather than basal reading schemes. These instructors believe that reading can and should be its own reward. The key to a successful reading program is in providing for a wide range of enriching, satisfying books and helping children to find their own rewards in these books.

The provision for worthwhile reading materials and time to read and talk about them are all very essential. In such a setting, the pupils are able to compare their individual reactions to books and in effect become a community of readers where books and understanding from books are shared. They learn what it is to be a lifelong reader.[1] A recent national commission regarding reading instruction made several recommendations relating to the importance of a literature-based reading curriculum. The following are some of the key conclusions of the study.[2]

**1. Children should spend more time in independent reading by reading a minimum of two hours per week at the third- or fourth-grade level. The books should include classics and modern works of fiction and nonfiction.**

**2. Schools should maintain well-stocked and managed libraries in order to assure a constant access for children to read a large number of interesting and informative books. A professional librarian is also important for encouraging young readers to read widely in books that match the interest and ability levels of the learners.**

In building a viable literature-based reading program for elementary children, a number of important principles and concepts should be kept in mind. Applying these ideas during the construction and implementation stages of the reading curriculum will help to insure the complete success of learners as they reach out to the goal of being informed and interested in all phases of the reading act.

**First, special reading programs that stress critical thinking and other skills should be implemented as appropriate.** For example, the *Junior Great Books Program* has been a part of the fourth grade curriculum of the Francis W. Parker School of Chicago for several years. While the program is utilized as a studies guide for gifted learners in many schools, it is employed with *all* pupils in the Parker School. The Great Book series has had a very positive impact on learners because it has enabled them to absorb and interpret the stories inferentially and has encouraged the expansion of ego and self-esteem.[3]

**Second, a large number of books at many interest and subject levels should be purchased.** Many authorities believe that at least four books should be purchased for each child enrolled in the program. For example, a class of 30 fourth-grade pupils should have access to at least 120 books. Some of these volumes could be a part of a series that are published by a number of reputable publishers. Examples of such series can be found in the appendices section of this volume. When purchasing these books such aspects as the following should be remembered: interests of the learners; their age groups; and the readability level of the volumes as determined by a reputable formulae such as the Fry, Smog, Flesch, and Dale-Chall.

**Third, a learning environment must be established that will help insure meaningful conversation, build new reading interests, and lessen individual comparison with other pupils.** Elementary teachers should learn as much as possible about their student's interests and attitudes through the use of verbal and written interest inventories. These data can be used for such decisions as grouping learners, arranging classroom furniture, and purchasing appropriate reading books. The total structure for the program should be one that allows the maximum amount of effort possible for a given learner to spend time reading, enjoy the physical surroundings, and possess a feeling of genuine happiness with the total experience.

**Fourth, a generous amount of time should be provided for the pupils to read.** Unfortunately, the total "reading time" allocated in a traditional basal approach classroom is designed primarily to teach a vast array of fragmented reading skills (with accompanying workbook assignments), and little, if any, time is given to recreational reading that correlates with the learner's interest and abilities. A period of uninterrupted silent sustained reading (USSR) amounting to as much as thirty minutes a day may be provided. Informal individual verbal conferences might be conducted to ask the learner certain questions regarding his/her reactions to such matters as the most exciting part of the selection and the nature of the plot or structure of the story. Various programs involving rewards may be used such as the Pizza Hut Corporation promotional program that provides a pizza lunch for pupils who read a certain number of books.

**Fifth, provisions must be made for pupils to talk to each other about their reading experiences and favorite books.** This type of sharing can occur in small groups or large groups when individual children can tell the entire class about the stories and selections they are currently reading. In a few instances, many successful teachers in a literature-based setting encourage pupils to show original illustrations they have made regarding different scenes in the story. They may also want to play the part of important story characters and portray exciting, humorous, and scary scenes.

Perhaps several children have read the same selection and wish to form a panel discussion to compare feelings and opinions regarding certain elements of a book or story. They could speculate about such matters as how *they* thought the story should have ended or if they felt the characters were honest, fair, and genuine.

**Sixth, there is an important place in literature-based environments for the assessing and monitoring of the reading skill component levels of individual elementary pupils.** Every competent teacher regardless of instructional orientation must necessarily be concerned about the degree of overall reading skill competency obtained by each student. A thorough, planned system of observation should yield valuable data regarding such matters as pupil attitudes, comprehension skill level abilities, and word attack proficiency.

Individual reading conferences are invaluable for checking reading skill progress since they provide a scenario whereby the teacher can ask questions dealing with such aspects as literal, interpretive, critical, and creative comprehension. Pupils may also be engaged in process writing during which time the pupils write creative stories utilizing a basic core of words that have been written on the board by the teacher.

It is even possible to use commercial individual reading tests such as the *Gray Oral Reading Test* for evaluating basic word attack skills. In all cases, the assessment procedures should be as "low-key" and nonthreatening as possible. If the activity is not conducted properly, interest in reading can be severely damaged. The goal of the elementary teacher should always be that of providing a secure environment where the discussion and sharing of books is always perceived as being a pleasurable experience.

In analyzing the total structure of a literature-based program that has been planned to be effective and innovative, several salient conclusions must be drawn.

1. Pupils, by and large, make responsible choices when selecting books. The major responsibility of the teacher is to supply a wide range of books for learners with minimum restriction as to the kinds of books chosen. It is not the role of the instructor to act as a complete censor for all reading.

2. Though it may appear that some pupils will never like reading, the enticing nature of being surrounded by dozens of exciting books is a strong attraction for even the most reluctant reader. The vision of seeing practically all of their friends reading and enjoying the experience is a strong motivator for all learners present to want to read. Finding out the preferences of reluctant readers and supplying them with appropriate books is a reasonable approach to help all children to read widely.

3. Uninterrupted silent reading periods can be successful if several guidelines are followed: (a) the teacher *reads* a book and *does not* correct papers; (b) there is a wide variety of high interest-low vocabulary books available on many reading levels; and (c) the USSR periods are regularly scheduled periods and not "something we get to do if we behave."

4. The reading conference (discussed earlier) must be well planned with interesting and penetrating questions designed for use with individual pupils. Questions such as the following may be used.
   (a) Which character did you like best?
   (b) Did you learn any lesson from the story that might help you to be a better person?
   (c) What was the most exciting part of the story?

5. Literature-based reading programs must be well planned with sufficient structure to assure that cognitive as well as affective skills are being developed. Careful records must be kept with regard to progress on basic reading skill development as well as kinds and the nature of books being read. Teachers are responsible for reporting progress in reading skills to all parents during parent-teacher conferences. Parents should be convinced that the reading curriculum is responsible, timely, and meeting the needs of their children.

6. One authority[4] notes that there are at least three important things that must be established during the first few weeks of a school term in a literature-based classroom. They are (a) a reading corner; (b) a changing class library; and (c) a supportive classroom for

reading. For the reading corner, the teacher may get a bulk loan of 50 or more books from the main school library for use in the reading corner. Every two weeks the books are returned and another set of books is obtained. The corner itself needs to be both comfortable and attractive with accompanying drapes and appropriate seats. The classroom atmosphere should be warm and positive and reading scheduled for at least one hour each day during which time the teacher reads aloud as many books as possible. He or she shares as many books as possible to build enthusiasm. During the reading time the pupils should read individually with meaningful conferences to follow.

In summary, a reading program that is literature-based allows pupils an opportunity to read widely in many different subject areas with an accompanying ever-growing level of overall skill development. Reading is thought of as an interesting, motivating activity that is student-centered instead of subject centered. The world of books comes alive for all elementary children regardless of their age, learning levels, and interests.

## ROLE OF COOPERATIVE LEARNING
## IN READING INSTRUCTION

In recent years much emphasis has been given to the role and function of cooperative learning as an adjunct activity for helping pupils build an increasing level of reading skills. The entire concept of cooperative learning encompasses a wide range of strategies for promoting academic learning through peer cooperation and communication. As the term "cooperative learning" implies, students help each other learn, share ideas and resources, and plan cooperatively what and how to study. The teachers do not dictate specific instructions but rather allows students varying degrees of choice as to the substance and goals of their learning activities, thus making students active participants in the process of acquiring knowledge.[5]

Persons who have used cooperative learning strategies in the area of reading have had much success because of several basic principles that they have followed in planning and implementing the total program. *First,* the reading instructional methods employed by the teacher must be guided toward the objective of placing all students of all levels into small groups for the purpose of working toward a common goal. The success of one student transfers toward helping a less able friend succeed—not the competitive atmosphere that so frequently pervades the traditional classroom.

*Second*, the successful planning that many teachers have used in past years to build laboratory and discussion groups for basically remedial purposes can be easily transferred to total class situations for the teaching of on-going basic skills instruction. In an environment whereby ability levels are individual pupils are de-emphasized and common goals are sought, pupils develop a far greater sense of positive self-concept and a feeling of personal success. The old axiom that "two heads are better than one" certainly applies to cooperative learning. Many more new and creative ideas originate in a cooperative learning setting than could ever be possible in a whole class competitive environment.

*Third*, cooperative learning programs can succeed at every class and learning level from the primary grades through the university levels. While it has been especially successful in the elementary grades, spectacular successes have been observed at the university level. Several noted programs have been in existence for at least 20 years. David DeVries of Johns Hopkins University developed the famous Student-Teams Achievement Divisions in the 1970s. The teams are composed of high, average, and below average students who represent a broad range of racial and ethnic backgrounds with the goal of forming a microcosm of the entire class. Competition is de-emphasized with the major attention given to the amount of improvement shown by each person.

*Fourth*, intergroup relations are drastically improved in cooperative learning environments because young students who learn cooperatively very often begin to respect every other person's importance as a contributing human being even though the individual may represent a minority ethnic group. Left to their own desires, most children of one race or ethnic group generally congregate with others of their same color or race. In cooperative learning programs, a true integrated learning group may well be the result. When pupils work closely together they very often find they have much more in common than they thought.

*Fifth*, the implementation of cooperative learning procedures does not require a special budget or monetary outlay. The elementary teacher needs only a minimum amount of training because the program requires only that learners may be assigned to small groups, provided appropriate teaching materials at their instructional levels, analyzed for overall performance, and provided a combination of extrinsic and intrinsic awards.

*Sixth*, teams should be established according to the students' abilities. Tom Bernagozzi[6] tried to ensure variety of experience and exposure by reshuffling the teams periodically. He changed the teams every six weeks to give the pupils a chance to be classmates with everyone in the class. Reshuffling also provides diversity if the class isn't balanced by race or gender. The teacher doesn't have to make a new list every time the teams are changed. Teachers should use their judgment to switch the high and low achievers.

Bernagozzi[7] notes that cooperative learning is easily adapted to any basal reading series or combination of reading materials. First, he split the four-member teams into pairs, making sure that the partners were at the same reading level. Comprehensive questions were then developed to encourage pupils to retell part of the story in their own words. Vocabulary was introduced and taught. Five quizzes were given involving comprehension, spelling, and reading skills. Individual and team scores were recorded. The *amount of improvement* was the major goal, not individual competitive scores. Through it all, he notes that his students enjoyed reading and really using their thinking skills.

An interesting cooperative learning program was recently undertaken in the Omaha, Nebraska Public Schools. Marian Warden, Editor of *"Frontier"* describes the program in the following manner.

> **They call themselves "The Smart Hearts."**
> **Each of 22 students in a fourth grade classroom had a role in selecting their class name last fall.**
> **"The Smart Hearts" are students at Field Club School. Their teachers use cooperative learning as an instructional technique.**
> **Dr. Harlan Rimmerman, assistant supervisor, Omaha Public Schools Department of Instruction, points out that cooperative learning helps students increase self-confidence and academic achievement.**
> **"In cooperative learning, students work together in groups of three or four," Dr. Rimmerman explains. "No student is successful until the group is successful. Cooperation—not competition—is rewarded."**
> **He points out that "cooperative learning students don't feel the stress of the normal classroom. This helps students become self-reliant," he says.**
> **Chapter I teacher Sharon Goetz and OPS teacher Sheila Riley coordinate plans for cooperative learning.**
> **They introduce new concepts. Then they work with "the other 22 teachers in the room."**
> **Mrs. Goetz explains that "students work together on projects. They discuss materials and explain them to each other."**
> **"A student is not encouraged to share a correct answer with a classmate,"**

Mrs. Goetz continues. "Rather, a student who knows how to find the correct answer shares the technique with a classmate."

The teachers say the program helps students develop leadership skills, creativity, and self-confidence.

This is illustrated by some of the names selected by learning groups in "The Smart Hearts" classroom. Group names include "Math Wizards" and "I Can Factory."[8]

Barbara Stoodt suggests at least six different methods of utilizing cooperative learning in reading classes. They are:

1. Students read aloud to one another, page by page, until a story is completed.
2. Students discuss a story the group has read silently. They should discuss answers and agree before responding (quiz-show style).
3. They map words or stories.
4. They do categorization activities.
5. Students do "think-alouds" while other group members identify the types of thinking used.
6. They engage in guided independent reading, which includes: asking and answering questions; paraphrasing content; outlining; mapping; summarizing; completing study guides; and dramatizing stories.[9]

There are numerous publications available to elementary teachers who would like help in establishing cooperative learning strategies in a reading program. Some of these are:

1. *Circles of Learning: Cooperation in the Classroom,* by David W. Johnson, Roger T. Johnson, Edythe Johnson Holubec, and Patricia Roy (Association for Supervision and Curriculum Development, 225 N. Washington St., Alexandria, VA 22314; revised edition, 1986).
2. *A Guidebook for Cooperative Learning: A Technique for Creating More Effective Schools,* by Dee Dishon and Pat Wilson O'Leary (Learning Publications, Inc. 5351 Gulf Dr., Holmes Beach, FL 34217, 1985).

Additional information may be secured from these sources.

1. The Center For Social Organization of Schools, The Johns Hopkins University, Dept. L88, 3505 N. Charles St., Baltimore, MD 21218 (301-338-7570).
2. The Cooperative Learning Center, 202 Pattee Hall, University of Minnesota, Dept. L88, Minneapolis, MN 55455 (612-624-7031).

## SUMMARY

Motivation is a key factor for any child or adult who is attempting to improve his or her level of reading ability. There are many causes for lack of motivation and these must be analyzed carefully. Specific techniques can help motivation levels considerably.

The infusion of a wide range of reading materials in a literature-based strategy allows pupils to become acquainted with numerous subjects at many different instructional levels. The many fundamental concepts that should be followed are carefully outlined in this chapter.

Cooperative learning has received wide attention in recent years as a strategy for helping children help each other. There are many different opportunities in an elementary reading class for these activities to take place. Many of them are described in this chapter.

## REFERENCES

1. Hancock, Joelie and Susan Hill (Editors). *Literature-Based Reading Programs At Work*, Portsmouth, New Hampshire, Heinemann, 1987, p. 1.
2. Commission on Reading. *Becoming A Nation of Readers*, Washington, D.C., National Institute of Education, 1984, p. 119.
3. Feiertag, Judy and Loren Chernoff. "Inferential Thinking and Self-Esteem Through The Junior Great Books Program," *Childhood Education*, V. 63, No. 4 (April, 1987), pp. 22–24.
4. Hancock and Hill, p. 13.
5. Sharan, Yael and Shlomo Sharan. "Training Teachers for Cooperative Learning," *Educational Leadership*, V. 45, No. 3 (November, 1987), p. 21.
6. Bernagozzi, Tom. "One Teacher's Approach," *Learning 88*, V. 16, No. 6 (February, 1988), p. 40.
7. Bernagozzi, pp. 42–43.
8. Warden, Marian. "Cooperative Learning Focus of Instruction," *Frontier* (March, 1989), p. 2.
9. Stoodt, Barbara D. *Reading Instruction* (Second Edition). New York, Harper & Row, 1989, p. 290.

## Chapter VIII

# EVALUATING THE
# ELEMENTARY READING PROGRAM

One of the most important segments of any viable reading program is that of **evaluation.** For reading instruction to be effective, a four-step approach to curriculum development must be undertaken. *First,* a precise outline of the desired reading competencies to be accomplished by a given group of students needs to be formulated. *Second,* a program of evaluation must be established which will yield data relative to the competency status of every student regarding **each** desired stated skill. *Third,* teaching strategies need to be devised to help learners develop each competency at a maximum level. *Fourth,* a final evaluation program needs to be devised to assess the proficiency of the teaching program. At the elementary school level this program should consist of both commercial and informal devices and strategies to help insure that all phases of the reading curriculum are involved. In whole language programs where a significant amount of cooperative learning activities are involved, anecdotal records as well as structured and unstructured visual and auditory methods should be employed. Many positive affective skills that are common to many whole language environments cannot be measured accurately by ordinary testing devices.

The elementary teacher is in a strategic position to conduct both continual and periodic evaluation of reading competencies. To give a proper perspective to the total area of evaluation, three important topics are discussed in this chapter. They are: the meaning of evaluation; strategies for measuring student reading achievement with informal devices; and guidelines for interpreting and utilizing test data.

## THE MEANING OF EVALUATION

Throughout the years since the establishment of private and public schools, the definition of evaluation as applied to the instructional setting has assumed several meanings. For some teachers, evaluation consists of administering a series of tests for the purposes of establishing a grade for a student in a particular class. According to Gronlund[1] the definition of evaluation from an instructional standpoint consists of **a systematic process of determining the extent to which instructional objectives are achieved by pupils.** He further believes that "measurement" is different from "evaluation" since measurement refers to particular scores on a test whereas evaluation is much more comprehensive and involves **every** facet of assessment both formal and informal.

Marksheffel[2] believes that evaluation should be defined as **an educated, honest, orderly attempt to judge the approximate achievement of a student in light of clearly defined goals.** For a program of reading evaluation to be effective, several conditions must be present in the school environment. They are (1) a clearly defined and established list of desired objectives for the reading curriculum; (2) a group of faculty members who understand their roles in developing reading competencies for individual students; (3) a commitment to approaching reading skills instruction from **a process** rather than a **subject** point of view; and (4) the knowledge of the strategies involved in a complete program of evaluation in a given classroom as well as for the total school.

It is important to understand that the process of evaluation is even more important at the upper grade levels because the range of differences in a given class will **increase** through the school year and from semester to semester as the child progresses through school. Zintz[3] further explains that if the range of reading ability in second grade is four years on standardized reading tests, it is to be expected that, with good teaching this range will, by the eighth grade, by about ten years.

Evaluation must be thought of in the broadest sense and should include such data as scores from achievement tests, teacher-made tests, and daily assignments; messages received from daily conversation with students; an assessment of an individual's attitude toward the act of reading obtained through the observation of verbal and nonverbal cues; and the determination of reading interests by listening to comments made by students during class sessions. An estimation of the child's status in the home environment can be judged from data in the school records, parent-teacher conferences, and information received from community and school leaders.

## Products of an Effective Reading Evaluation Program

If a reading evaluation program is functioning at a maximum level, several important products should be realized. Some of these outgrowths are as follows:

1. **Identifies** those students who may be considered exceptional in nature such as the gifted and retarded reader.
2. **Aids** teachers and administrators in the process of grouping pupils which will result in maximum reading achievement for each student.
3. **Determines** the degree and level of reading achievement attained by individual students as well as the accomplishments of the total group.
4. **Pinpoints** the areas of reading skill development which need to be improved in such components as word attack, vocabulary, comprehension, and resource reading skills.
5. **Provides** significant information to the school counselor and/or school psychologist as they attempt to devise a program of personal improvement for those students who may have antisocial behaviors.
6. **Suggests** methods or techniques which may be used to alter the existing curriculum to allow for better reading skill growth rates by students of varying abilities.
7. **Establishes** a bank of data which will help each teacher assign a reasonable grade for a specific content area.
8. **Identifies** certain students who may be underachievers and others who may not be performing at their potential levels.
9. **Provides** significant data for teachers in determining names of pupils who need special small group instruction in a whole language classroom.
10. **Creates** a body of information for teachers for deciding who should be involved in cooperative learning situations.

## Important Guidelines for Reading Evaluation

As the reading evaluation program is constructed, there are several important guidelines or principles which should be kept in mind. If these are given priority during the construction of the evaluation strategies, the amount of positive help for both pupils and teachers will be greatly enhanced. The following are eight of the most significant aspects to remember.

1. **The most important purpose of evaluation is to improve instruction.** As Durkin[4] notes, we should use what is learned to make future instructional decisions. In many situations, data from testing programs are recorded in a child's permanent record and little use is made of the information for improving instruction. Teachers should remember that an analysis of evaluation data may reveal the inescapable fact that a change is necessary in the method of teaching various lessons. The results of an achievement test may, for example, demonstrate a need for greater emphasis in comprehension or vocabulary. Effective teachers use the diagnostic process to guide them in utilizing the most desirable methods for insuring maximum growth in reading for each student.

2. **The purpose of the evaluative procedures should be made clear to the students.** Pupils are an integral part of the process of assessment and optimum performance can only be expected when the learner understands that the data from the evaluative procedures will be used to improve the learning environment for him or her. Aulls[5] is of the opinion that the directions for the test should be carefully explained to facilitate maximum performance on the part of the learner. If students understand that the evaluation efforts are designed to benefit their personal reading abilities, they will be more prone to exhibit their best efforts when marking tests.

3. **Evaluation should be approached from a broad definition.** As noted earlier, evaluation consists of much more than the mere administration and scoring of a limited number of commercial and standardized tests. Informal tests like those described later in this chapter can form an important part of the evaluation process since they test aspects of the reading act which **may not** be found on many of the more common commercial tests. Valuable pieces of data can be obtained from conversations and dialogue with students.

4. **Evaluation must be thought of as a continuous process as well as a periodic endeavor.** To secure the most meaningful information about a pupil's ability in reading requires **daily** assessments of his or her performance in such important areas as word attack, comprehension, and vocabulary. Lessons need to be constructed which are based on the student's **current** evaluative data about the

learner's skill level competency, preferred learning modality, and attitudes with respect to reading. Daily interaction with the student which involves assessment of skill development through meaningful daily assignments will help to provide information that will aid the instructor in preparing lessons which will be individualized and designed to meet a specific instructional need without having to wait for the results of a periodic achievement test. Keeping examples of a pupil's daily work are helpful in explaining the student's academic progress during the parent-teacher conference period. By analyzing diagnostic results from both periodic and continuous techniques, the teacher and parent will have a better overall view of the pupil's school progress in the important area of reading.

5. **An evaluation of a pupil's reading skill development should be made from studying patterns of scores from several testing strategies.** To arrive at the conclusion that a student is deficient in word attack skills demands that this information be based on the results of **several** tests. A learner may do poorly on one given test because of physical or emotional stress. In the area of vocabulary, one may wish to analyze the results from the vocabulary section of the annual achievement test; information obtained from a series of teacher-made vocabulary tests; and the analysis of speaking vocabulary by listening to the conversations and class discussion of the reader during daily class periods. Since the validity of any **one** test may be open to question, the study of a total pattern of scores is both useful and imperative.

6. **One should conduct evaluative procedures in the most competent and thorough manner as possible.** All commercial tests require that specific directions be followed in the use of diagnostic and achievement tests. The test becomes invalid if the directions are not followed precisely. Teachers **need to become very familiar with all of the procedures before attempting to administer any kind of test. To secure the most valid and reliable tests, one should consult such sources as the** *Mental Measurements Yearbooks, Tests In Print*, or *Reading Tests and Reviews* before selecting instruments which are to be used for major evaluative purposes. Information assessments of the value of given tests may also be obtained from fellow classroom teachers or administrators who have used certain tests. These data can help in establishing the face validity of such instruments.

7. **A variety of commercial and informal evaluative devices should be employed in an all-inclusive reading analysis program.** Because of the fact that different tests have varied strengths and limitations, it is imperative for the content teacher to utilize testing instruments which are valid for a myriad of purposes and emphasis. By and large, commercial reading achievement tests perform most satisfactorily in evaluating vocabulary, comprehension, and rate of reading. There are several affective domain areas such as **love of reading** and **reading interests** which can only be assessed through a careful study of a pupil's oral discussions and class recitations. One of the chief limitations of informal devices is that they are not standardized with national norms. Teachers must recognize that all strategies have both advantages and limitations for use in evaluating cognitive, affective, and psychomotor skill competencies.

8. **A careful record should be maintained of all of the results obtained from evaluative devices.** A file should be maintained for each student which indicates the degree to which the individual has mastered certain designated reading skill competencies. Critical scores could be established for each skill to insure that mastery has been completed as validated by specific testing devices. The total record can be utilized to help the teacher design the exact instructional program which may be needed by the student. This information is also helpful in the conduct of parent-teacher conferences.

In summary, **the major purpose of evaluation is to improve instruction.** A varied assortment of evaluation strategies should be used and the purpose of each device should be made known to the learner. The pattern of scores should be studied and the total results used to help improve the educational climate for the reader.

## STRATEGIES FOR MEASURING STUDENT READING ACHIEVEMENT WITH INFORMAL DEVICES

As noted earlier, an evaluation program should be composed of a number of different devices which include both commercial and informal measures. Informational devices such as those described in this section can be used in a variety of situations, are easily scored, and constructed with relatively little difficulty. Directions are not standardized and thus can be adapted to meet a particular instructional situation.

They should be utilized with those students who are not functioning at desired levels of reading competency.

The strategies or devices described in the following section are classroom tested, easily compiled, and can be functional in both individual and class-wide settings. Data can be gained from the instruments which will help the teacher to group pupils, utilize the proper book with a given reader, and fashion group instruction which will help the total class increase proficiency in the basic reading skill areas. Individual tests should be given generally to those who are reading at much below grade level but have a potential for reading at or above grade level. The directions for constructing and administering the test are outlined in some detail and should be followed carefully to facilitate maximum validity and reliability levels.

## The Subjective Reading Inventory

The Subjective Reading Inventory is a very useful instrument for use with individual students in assessing oral reading, word attack, and vocabulary. Comprehension proficiencies at the literal, interpretive, and critical levels can also be assessed. The results of the inventory can be used quite profitably in finding the most appropriate textbook to use with a given student.

The construction of the inventory involves the use of selections from a graded series of books. One should find books which are written about three grade levels above and three grade levels below the grade level of the student being tested. If the teacher is going to use the material with a seventh-grade student, selections should be employed from books written at the fourth-, fifth-, sixth-, seventh-, eighth-, ninth-, and tenth-grade levels.

For the **oral reading aspect** of the test, select a 100-word passage from the first third of each book and ask the student to read it aloud. For complete accuracy, tape the reading and then listen carefully and record all substitutions, omissions, and repetitions. Each error counts one percentage point wrong. If the student reads the material with 95 to 97 percent accuracy, the grade level of the material may be considered the instructional reading level of the student. If a score of less than 95 percent is obtained, the next **lower** level of material should be used until a score of 95 to 97 percent is obtained. If a score of more than 95 percent is earned on the first test, the next **higher** level should be utilized until the 95 to 97 percent score is realized.

For the **silent reading comprehension portion** of the test, select a 300-word passage from each of the books for the student to read silently. The selection should come from the second half of the book being employed. Compile four or five questions for each selection. Some questions should deal with details, other with the main idea, while some may involve critical reading or drawing conclusions. If five questions are used, a weight of 20 percentage points should be given to each question. For the material to be at the instructional reading level, the student must answer four of the five questions accurately. If **all** questions are answered correctly, the questions from the next **higher** level book should be used. If three or fewer questions are answered, the next **lower** level book should be used.

The level where the student scores four questions correct on the silent reading comprehension test should be considered the student's reading instructional level regardless of the level achieved on the oral reading part of the test. Many times, because of test anxiety or other reasons, the oral reading score may be lower than the silent reading comprehension measure. Since silent reading comprehension is the end product of reading, the comprehension score takes precedence over the oral reading measure. (The errors noted in the oral reading can be a **helpful** clue to the teacher in planning later reading lessons for the student.)

The results of the Subjective Reading Inventory can be most useful in determining if a given textbook is suitable for use with a certain student. If, for example, the readability of the book is at the ninth-grade level and a student scores at the ninth-grade instructional reading level on the test, one can assume that the text is suitable for that student. The level of the text should match the instructional reading level of the student for **maximum** learning to take place. (In far too many cases, the reading level of the textbook is higher than the true instructional reading level of the learner. When such a situation occurs, there is ultimate frustration and anxiety for the student.)

## Individual Sight Word Vocabulary Inventory

One of the most important aspects of reading is the degree of vocabulary power possessed by each student. The following inventory is designed to provide information relative to a given pupil's level of sight word vocabulary.

The first step in building the inventory is to find texts which are written at several grade levels. A seventh-grade teacher should find books which are at the fourth-, fifth-, sixth-, seventh-, eighth-, ninth-, and tenth-grade levels. Select a chapter or unit of material near the middle of the book. Beginning with the first word of each chapter, take each **tenth** word thereafter and place it in a column until 50 words have been written. These words should be double-spaced in pica type and placed on a strip of heavy paper. Some words may appear more than once. If this happens, use the eleventh or ninth word in some instances so the final list of 50 words will each be different.

A critical score of 45 should be established for each of the lists. If the student scores **more** than 47 proceed to the next **higher** grade level list. If the score is **less** than 45, proceed to the next **lower** grade level list. Continue the administration of the test until a score of 45–47 is obtained. One may conclude tentatively that the instructional reading level of the student with regard to vocabulary is at the level where the critical score was obtained on the *Individual Sight Word Vocabulary Inventory.*

**The materials used by the student in a given class should be at the critical level obtained on the test.** An analysis of the words mispronounced by the student can lend important clues regarding possible problems with phonics and other word attack areas. This information can be used to plan lessons which will be helpful in aiding the student improve his/her sight word vocabulary.

Though this test is designed for individual use, the words can be placed on a transparency and used on the overhead projector for utilization with small groups. If a teacher aide or student teacher is available, they can administer the test to individual students who are having general reading difficulties in the classroom.

## The Incomplete Sentences Test

Information concerning a pupil's attitudes and views toward reading can be obtained from administering this test and analyzing the responses. The sample items below are useful for middle- and upper-grade students. They may need to be altered for use with primary or secondary students. A total of 10 to 20 statements should be used for the exercise. The following are examples of questions which may be used:

1. Reading is _____.
2. The most difficult part of school is _____.
3. When I read books _____.
4. I hope I can _____.
5. Reading class assignments are _____.
6. The textbook for this class is _____.

When administering the test, one needs to assure the students that the information written on the sheets will be held in confidence. What they write will help the teacher to know them better so he/she can aid them with their assignments. The students should respond to all items, but if they choose not to answer certain items, they should have that option. If the reading difficulties of a student are such that they cannot read the items, they can be read orally in an individual conference and the responses noted by the teacher.

## GUIDELINES FOR INTERPRETING AND UTILIZING TEST DATA

During the school year teachers and counselors compile a large amount of test data which relate to such aspects as grade equivalents, percentiles, scaled scores, and similar kinds of information. The information provided by computer test scoring services is often voluminous and frightening to many teachers. These data can be valuable to instructors if these guidelines are followed.

1. **Study the commercial test administrator's manual carefully to derive accurate information relative to the meaning of certain aspects of the test.** If further information is needed, visit with the company representative. The school counselor or psychologist may also supply needed information. A careful understanding of the meaning of terms is important to insure that correct interpretations of the test are given to both students and their parents.

2. **The analysis of the meaning of a test score should be made in the context of a pupil's background of experience, physical and emotional deficiencies, and other factors.** In some cases, a learner's emotional and/or physical status may create an abnormally low score on a test. The conditions may be so limiting that the test score would have questionable value. Progress in an academic environment may be minimal for these individuals.

3. **An item analysis of achievement tests should be made to determine the exact skill areas where the student is deficient.** For example, one may determine that the learner needs directed lessons in phonics, literal level comprehension, and vocabulary. The results of the test can be used for formulating the exact lessons needed by students to facilitate improvement of reading skills.

## SUMMARY

An effective program of evaluation is useful for a number of reasons. The most important purpose of evaluation is to improve instruction. Total evaluation consists of a number of aspects including commercial tests, informal devices, and observation of the student in a number of situations. There are many informal tests like those described in this chapter which can be highly useful in deriving valuable data concerning a learner's reading ability. The correct interpretation of the meaning of test data is important if correct decisions are to be made regarding a student's future educational program.[6]

## REFERENCES

1. Gronlund, Norman E. *Measurement and Evaluation in Teaching* (Fourth Edition). New York, Macmillan, Inc., 1981, pp. 5–6.
2. Marksheffel, Ned D. *Better Reading in The Secondary School — Principles and Practices for Teachers.* New York, Ronald Press, 1966, p. 79.
3. Zintz, Miles V. *Corrective Reading* (Third Edition). Dubuque, William C. Brown, 1977, p. 27.
4. Durkin, Dolores, *Teaching Them To Read* (Fourth Edition). Boston, Allyn and Bacon, 1983, p. 437.
5. Aulls, Mark W. *Developing Readers in Today's Elementary School.* Boston, Allyn and Bacon, 1982, p. 592.
6. The material in this chapter is an adaptation of: Chapter 3, *Improving Reading Skills in The Content Area* by Donald C. Cushenbery and published by Charles C Thomas, Publisher, Springfield, Illinois, 1985. Reprinted by permission.

# APPENDIX A

# INSTRUCTIONAL MATERIALS FOR READING IMPROVEMENT

This list is a sample of available materials which may assist an elementary teacher in the teaching of reading skills. The listing of an item does not necessarily imply a personal endorsement of the author for a given selection. The use of a material on a pilot basis may be a practical procedure to employ. Complete addresses for the publishers can be found in Appendix B.

## COMPREHENSION

| Publisher | Title | Grade Level | Description |
|---|---|---|---|
| Curriculum Associates, Inc. | Clues for Better Reading | 2–9 | This program is designed to provide intensive reading comprehension practice in a variety of content areas. |
| Curriculum Associates, Inc. | Listening Comprehension Skills Program | 1–10 | Four kits comprise this program which offers practice in the eleven major comprehension skills area. |
| Educators Publishing Service | Reading Comprehension in Varied Subject Matter | 1–12 | Each workbook follows the same format of a selection followed by comprehension-check exercises. |
| EMC Publishing | Easy-to-Read Classics | 2–4 | This set was created to provide a literature course for upper-grade, low-level readers. Comprehension questions conclude each chapter. |
| Jamestown | Comprehension Skills Series | 6–8 | A cassette accompanies the graded booklets which review comprehension skills. |
| Prentice-Hall | Comprehension Plus | 1–6 | A complete curriculum for comprehension skills instruction is included in this multi-level workbook series. |

| | | | |
|---|---|---|---|
| Random House | Random Reading Almanacs | 3–6 | Each of the six almanacs is keyed to a specific comprehension skill and is written in an attractive adult format to stimulate interest. |
| Reader's Digest Services | Reader's Workshop | 3–7 5–9 | Ninety self-directing lesson provide sequential instruction of twenty-five comprehension skills. |
| Scholastic, Inc. | Scholastic Bookshelf | 4–6 | Four vital comprehension areas are featured in each kit of outstanding juvenile fiction and non-fiction. |
| Steck-Vaughn | Pinpoint Critical Reading Skills Series | 4–6 | The Pinpoint Series concentrate on the development of the comprehension skills which involve thinking, reasoning, and judging. |
| Teachers College Press | Gates-Peardon-LaClair Reading Exercises | 1–6 | Nine self-correcting books compose this series which focuses on the development of reading comprehension skills. |

## COMPUTER PROGRAMS

| Publisher | Title | Grade Level | Description |
|---|---|---|---|
| American Educational Computer, Inc. | Micro-Read, Apple II | 1–8 | Micro-Read is a reading skills support program that covers all reading skills. |
| American Guidance Service | MicroSoc Thinking Games | | The computer programs are content rich, yet easy-to-operate games. The software helps your child understand language concepts and develop vital problem solving abilities. |
| Barnell Loft, Ltd. | Reading Through the Fourth Dimension | 4–12 | These computer programs are very useful for providing enrichment or independent practice. The two diskettes include some of the following: pronouns—personal, interrogative, indefinite signal |

| | | | words, and cause and effect sequences. |
|---|---|---|---|
| Barnell Loft, Ltd. | Word Theater | 4–9 | In this fine software package There are a total of eight diskettes. Each diskette has a total of 150 skits that are designed to improve comprehension vocabulary and writing skills. |
| Borg-Warner Educational Systems | Critical Reading, Apple II | 4–6 | The rules of logic which are fundamental to the development of critical reading and thinking skills are taught in this individualized program. |
| Brain Bank, Inc. | Four Basic Reading Skills, Commodore PET, Apple II, TRS-80 | 5–12 | How to recall details, identify the main idea, draw conclusions, and arrange things sequentially are the skills reviewed in this program. |
| Computer Assisted Instruction, Inc. | Elementary Reading Efficiency System Apple II, TRS-80, Franklin 100, Commodore PET | 2–6 | Although written on a lower grade level, this individualized program is meant for upper elementary students and is intended to expand pupil's vocabularies and advance student's abilities to read for meaning. |
| Computer Assisted Instruction, Inc. | K–12 Reading Efficiency System Apple II, TRS-80, Franklin, Commodore PET | K–12 | Review of the basic phonic principles is provided by this program which should enable the student to build reading vocabulary. |
| Computer Island | Context Clues Series, TRS-80 | 4–6 | Fifty situational paragraphs are followed by questions which require the users to find the correct answers from the context. |
| The Continental Press, Inc. | Cause and Effect | 3–5 | A fascinating computer program that develops cause and effect relationships |
| The Continental Press, Inc. | Extra! Extra! | Ages 8 and up | The computer helps students to uncover the "facts" for a news- |

|  |  |  |  |
|---|---|---|---|
|  |  |  | paper story. This unique program offers three skill levels and over 60 different news stories. The objective is to encourage quick, accurate fact finding. |
| The Continental Press, Inc. | Fact or Opinion | 2–3.5 | A game board format provides a unique format that helps students make distinctions between facts and opinions. |
| The Continental Press, Inc. | Speed Reader II | 7 and up | Six lessons are provided in this computer program that will train students in established techniques for increasing reading speed and proficiency. |
| Creative Curriculum Inc./ Computer Course- ware, Inc. | Alaskan Gold, Apple II | 9 | A skillbook accompanies this program which was designed to improve study skills, reading comprehension, perceptual training, and vocabulary knowledge. |
| Follett Library Book Co. | Alphakey | K–3 | Young students will enjoy learning the alphabet on the computer's keyboard. After typing the correct letter, the child is rewarded with a smiling face. There is no attempt to teach finger position. |
| Follett Library Book Co. | Juggles' Rainbow | Pre-school | Disguised as fun in this com- puter program are pre-reading skills and computer basics. They will be learning the con- cepts of above/below and left/ right as they generate patterns with the graphics. |
| Follett Library Book Co. | Letter Recognition | K–1 | This program not only intro- duces the child to the computer but also helps develop letter recognition. The program options include upper case letters only, lower case letters only, numerals, or mixed characters. |

| | | | |
|---|---|---|---|
| Follett Library Books Co. | Opposites | 1–10 | Designed to increase your child's vocabulary this computer program can use the words provided or you can add your own words. |
| Follett Library Books Co. | Reading for Meaning with Mother Goose | 2–4 | The two programs disks include over 60 separate rhymes. The question section requires the child to identify details, sequence of events, predict outcomes and identify main ideas. |
| Follett Library Books Co. | Wizard of Words | 1–12 | Using a powerful dictionary of over 38,000 words, this computer program has five different word games to improve your child's language learning skills. |
| Learning Well | Behind-The-Wheel Program, Apple II | 2–5 | Behind-the-Wheel Programs are enrichment activities which focus on following directions. |
| Learning Well | What Comes First, Apple II | 2–5 | What Comes First is a two-level enrichment activity which is intended to reinforce the skill of putting events in sequential order. |
| Micro School Programs | The Reader, TRS, 80 | 1–8 | The Reader is a variable speed reading program for students to read passages and answer follow-up questions. |
| Micograms, Inc. | Professor Snead, Commodore 64, Commodore PET | 5–9 | Professor Snead is a series of twelve reading programs which check comprehension while increasing a student's reading rate. |
| Milliken | Cloze Plus Apple II | 3–8 | Cloze Plus is a program for the development of vocabulary and comprehension skills through structured cloze and context analysis activities. |
| Milliken | Comprehension Power Apple II | 4–12 | Each diskette contains three stories which provide practice and measurement of the basic comprehension skills. |

| Milton Bradley | All About What You Read, Apple II | 4–8 | All About What You Read is a comprehensive program designed to improve reading comprehension. |
| Milton Bradley | All About Words Apple II | 4–8 | All About Words uses Milton, the Wizard, to show pupils how to determine the meaning of unfamiliar words. |
| Milton Bradley | Reading Comprehension: Main Ideas and Details Apple II | 6–8 | Students practice listing the details and summarizing the main ideas of selections in this program. |
| Orange Cherry Media | Adventures Around the World, Commodore PET, TRS-80, Atari | 3–6 | Adventures Around the World is a reading skills development series. |
| The Psychology Corporation | Reading I, Apple II | 3–5 | Word identification, comprehension, and study skills are developed by the Reading I Program. |
| Radio Shack | Frankenstein TRS-80 | 4–6 | Frankenstein is a complete learning package that includes a diskette, a teacher's manual, student books, and a read-along cassette. |
| Scott, Foresman | Reading Wonders Apple II, Atari, TRS-80 | 5–7 | Reading Wonders is a program created to aid students in identifying the differences in style between fiction and non-fiction. |
| Wise Owl Workshop | Winning With Phonics, Apple II, TRS-80, Commodore 64 | 4–8 | Winning With Phonics uses exercises and games to teach phonics. |

## GENERAL READING PROGRAMS

| Publisher | Title | Grade Level | Description |
|---|---|---|---|
| American Guidance Service | High Hat Early Reading Programs | Pre-school to Grade 1 | This series makes possible a wealth of coordinated visual and verbal activities. Children learn to articulate single sounds correctly and blend sounds into syllables and words. |

| | | | |
|---|---|---|---|
| AV Concepts Corporation | Contained Reading Series | K–6 | More efficient and fluent reading is developed by this program which contains a workbook and a filmstrip for each level. |
| Barnell Loft, Ltd. | Developing Key Concepts in Comprehension | 1–10 | This exciting series stresses four key classes of ideas; identical, related, unrelated, and contradictory ideas. The series not only enhances their reading ability but also their ability to write with clarity. |
| Barnell Loft, Ltd. | New Specific Skills Series | 1–6 | Eight crucial reading skills are targeted for development in this program that contains fourteen levels of difficulty. |
| Croft, Inc. | Skillpacks | K–6 | Skillpacks is a complete, sequential program which is divided into subskill areas where all the activities are presented in order to master that objective. |
| Curriculum Associates, Inc. | Reading Skills Center | K–6 | There are three levels of Reading Skills Centers and each one contains a variety of activities which can be used individually or in small groups. |
| Educational Activities, Inc. | Flightpath to Reading | 2–4 | High interest and low vocabulary level are two appropriate descriptive phrases that fit the Flightpath series which was designed to be motivational. |
| Educational Activities, Inc. | I Hate To Read Series | K–6 | These short, humorous stories were created to stimulate and motivate reluctant readers. |
| EMC Publishing | Reading/Fiction | 4–9 | Reading/Fiction is a series of exciting stories, cassettes, and skill sheets which are written at the third grade level but will interest older pupils. |
| EMC Publishing | Real People at Work Reading | 5–12 | Each book has an accompanying cassette and workbook which |

| | Skills Program | | assists the reader in this series of interesting stories on a controlled reading level. |
|---|---|---|---|
| EMC Publishing | Science Readers | 4–9 | Different creatures are featured in each Science Reader set which are written on the third grade level but are intended for older students. |
| Fearon Teacher Aids | The Creativity Catalog | 4–8 | The gifted child will love the 30 projects for creating cartoons, picture books, and T.V. shows as well as the practical information about careers in acting, writing, and much more. |
| Ginn | Ginn Literature Series | 7–8 | Each unit is designed to instruct the junior high school student on how to read various forms of more sophisticated literature. |
| Good Apple | Super Sheets | 1–6 | Super Sheets workbooks strive to improve the student's basic reading skills through self-directing activity sheets. |
| Jamestown | Attention Span Stories | 6–9 | All of these exciting stories are written on the second and third grade levels, but intended to interest reluctant junior high school readers. |
| Laidlaw | The Laidlaw Reading Program | 1–8 | This is a basic developmental program that aims to help pupils become successful life-time readers. |
| Pendulum Press, Inc. | Read Along Program | 4–12 | The Read Along Program is a series of reading kits which contain books and coordinated workbooks on a variety of subjects. |
| Prentice-Hall | Phoenix Reading Series | 4–8 | The Phoenix Reading Series is a remedial reading program for intermediate and junior high students which systematically reteaches the basic reading skills. |

| | | | |
|---|---|---|---|
| Random House | The Random House Reading Program | 2–8 | This is a comprehensive reading program which promotes independent reading by using a variety of materials and selections from the best-loved childrens books. |
| Random House | Read-On | 1–4 | Read-On is a self-correcting simple diagnostic program that allows students to pinpoint their weaknesses. |
| Random House | Spotlight on Literature | 3–6 | Six collections of selections from America's most famous authors compose "Spotlight on Literature." |
| Reader's Digest Services | Skillbuilders | 1–12 | "Skillbuilders" are multi-level kits which are intended to expand and revitalize basal reading programs. |
| Scholastic, Inc. | Individualized Reading from Scholastic | 1–6 | Scholastic has created several kits on different reading levels that incorporate a variety of materials which will facilitate individualized reading instruction. |
| Scholastic, Inc. | Pleasure Reading Libraries | K–12 | Fifty books were selected for each grade level which fosters the enjoyment of reading through the "Pleasure Reading Libraries." |
| Scholastic, Inc. | Plus Reading | 2–6 | "Plus Reading" is meant to be a supplemental unit of fine children's literature which will challenge the better reader. |
| Scholastic, Inc. | Project Achievement: Reading | 9–12 | This project was carefully researched to give high school students reading as low as second-grade level the important skills necessary for taking standardized tests. |
| Scholastic, Inc. | Reluctant Reader and Easy Access Libraries | | The books in these libraries were carefully selected to appeal to upper-grade, slower readers. |

| | | | |
|---|---|---|---|
| | | | Each library kit contains 50 books. |
| Scholastic, Inc. | Scholastic Go: Reading in the Content Area | 4–8+ | "Scholastic Go" is a program that aims to help below-grade readers cope with on-grade level reading in content area textbooks. |
| Scholastic, Inc. | Scholastic Literature Units | 5–9 | The "Scholastic Literature Units" are intended to spur pupils into reading and writing excitement. |
| Scholastic, Inc. | Sprint Libraries | 4–6 | The "Sprint Libraries" were created to provide the middle-school, below-grade level reader with a positive supplemental reading experience. |
| Scholastic, Inc. | Sprint Reading Skills Program | 1–5 | The advertisements for this program claims that it contains all that a teacher will need to get even the poorest readers to almost grade level. |
| Scholastic, Inc. | Tune Into Books | 2–9 | Tune Into Books is a new collection of books for each grade level that are structured to provide sustained silent reading. |
| Scott, Foresman | Basics in Reading Program | K–8 | This is a basal reading program which provides materials for thorough skills instruction and lively reading experiences. |
| Scott, Foresman | The New Open Highways Program | K–8 | This program was created to spot weaknesses and to build skills while using a high interest content to prevent failure. |
| Scott, Foresman | Reading Unlimited Program | K–8 | Reading Unlimited is a program meant to give opportunities for concept and vocabulary growth through a multi-level system. |
| Scott, Foresman | Signal Series | 7–8 | The Signal Series is a total reading program for the junior high level hat alternates literature units with skill sections. |

| Steck-Vaughn | Mastering Basic Reading Skills | 2–6 | The Mastering Basic Reading Skills program is targeted for middle-grade students who are reading below grade level. |
| Sunburst Communications | Reading for Every Day: Survival Skills | 4–7 | This kit of 50 activity cards provides practice of the functional reading skills necessary for survival in everyday life. |
| Walt Disney Media | Auto Racing: Something for Everyone | 5–8 | Auto Racing is a filmstrip and book kit which is designed to motivate the reluctant reader. |
| Walt Disney Media | Movie Script Reading | 5–8 | Movie Script Reading uses film-strips, cassettes, scripts, and a teacher's guide to form an integrated approach to motivate the older reader. |
| Walt Disney Media | Reading Adventures | 4–8 | Reading Adventures presents captivating story topics with a low vocabulary level in order to stimulate the interest of the older, slower reader. |
| Winston Press | Power Reading | 1–12 | Power Reading is a file of reading skill units which focus on specific behavioral objectives and is intended to be a problem solver due to its complete diagnostic/prescriptive approach. |

## WORD ATTACK

| Publisher | Title | Grade Level | Description |
| --- | --- | --- | --- |
| Addison-Wesley | The Target Reading Skills Program | K–6 | This program is a set of audio-tapes. Each lesson has a target objective that develops a word attack skill. |
| Barnell Loft, Ltd. | Supportive Reading Skills: Word Recognition Program | K–6 | The basic word recognition skills are featured in this multilevel, colorful set which incorporates a variety of strategies and techniques. |
| Curriculum Associates, Inc. | Context Phonetic Clues | 3–6 | The improvement of word analysis skills by the inter- |

| | | | |
|---|---|---|---|
| | | | mediate level student is the focus of the Context Phonetic Clues Program. |
| Curriculum Associates, Inc. | Reading Skills Practice Kits | 2–8 | The Reading Skills Practice Kits are a collection of activity cards which reinforce the mastery of skills that are necessary for reading fluency. |
| Curriculum Associates, Inc. | Vocabulary: Fluency Program | 4–9 | Two student workbooks were developed to form this program which concentrates on review of the basic word attack skills. |
| Curriculum Associates, Inc. | Word Analysis Kit | 1–4 | Self-directing and self-correcting lesson cards which review the basic phonetic analysis skills were compiled to create this kit. |
| DLM Teaching Resources | Phonics in Context | 1–6 | Phonics in Context is a complete phonics program that stresses decoding skills. |
| DLM Teaching Resources | Sound Foundation Program | 1–6 | The Sound Foundations Programs are four systematically-planned programs that were developed to improve the vital word attack skills which promote reading improvement. |
| Education Activities, Inc. | Read/Language Game Box | K–6 | All of the components for each game are included in this box of developmental games that follow the growth of phonics and language skills. |
| Educators Publishing Service, Inc. | Explode the Code | 1–5 | Explode the Code is a workbook and activity sheet program that focuses on instructing students in the basic phonic concepts. |
| Educators Publishing Service, Inc. | Primary Phonics | K–4 | Primary Phonics is a structured phonetic approach to the teaching of reading which offers a flexible, individualized format. |
| Midwest Publications | Klooz | Non-Graded | Klooz is a game which was created to improve reading and thinking skills. Players are to |

|  |  |  | complete a paragraph with as few clues as possible. |
|---|---|---|---|
| Prentice-Hall | Phonics Plus | K–3 | Phonics Plus is a comprehensive word study program that provides for sequential skills development. |
| Scholastic, Inc. | Phonics Workbook | 1–3 | The most regular phonics elements necessary for decoding and using words in context are presented in the Phonics Workbooks where each workbook concentrates on a specific skill. |
| Steck-Vaughn | Sounds, Words, and Meanings | 1–6 | Instruction and practice in phonics are provided in the Sounds, Words, and Meanings workbooks. |

# ANNOTATED PROFESSIONAL BOOK LIST FOR ELEMENTARY READING TEACHERS

1. Alexander, J. Estelle (Editor). *Teaching Reading.* (Third Edition). Glenview, Illinois, Scott, Foresman & Company, 1988.

   This hardback edition relates to all phases of reading instruction. The information compiled by numerous selected reading authorities is especially valuable since the topics are described in light of the latest research findings coupled with easy-to-follow teaching suggestions. The relationship of writing and the other language arts is emphasized throughout all of the chapters presented.

2. Alexander, J. Estelle and Betty Heathington. *Assessing and Correcting Classroom Reading Problems.* Glenview, Illinois, Scott, Foresman and Company, 1988.

   This new text is especially useful to elementary teachers since the authors address affective, physical, and cultural factors and offer a wealth of proven classroom strategies that can be easily used by all elementary teachers. The busy classroom teacher will find the volume most helpful since the strategies are developed in a setting that is similar to many that are found in most elementary buildings.

3. Aulls, Mark W. *Developmental and Remedial Reading in the Middle Grades* (Abridged Edition). Boston, Allyn and Bacon, 1978.

   The book contains many useful ideas for the content area teacher wanting to adapt instruction to below grade level students. The conceptual framework and content of this book is designed to facilitate learning new ways to work with students.

4. Barr, Rebecca and Marilyn Sadow. *Reading Diagnosis for Teachers.* White Plains, New York, Longman, 1985.

   Every classroom teacher needs a handbook to be used to deal with the realities of individual reading levels of students. This is such a book. It gives usable diagnostic guidelines and procedures for the secondary classroom teacher, and helps teachers set goals and expectations that are consistent with a classroom program.

5. Baumann, Jane F. (Editor). *Teaching Main Idea Comprehension.* Newark, Delaware, International Reading Association, 1986.

   The author's emphasis in the eleven chapters in this book is teaching comprehension in many settings. The chapters have been written with the practitioner in mind, and each author has taken considerable effort to discuss instructional implications.

6. Cheyney, Arnold B. *Teaching Reading Skills Through the Newspaper.* Newark, Delaware, International Reading Association, 1984.

   This is one of the International Reading Association's service bulletins written to give specific help to classroom teachers. It can be read in one sitting and covers all of the basic premises of using the newspaper to teach reading vocabulary, speaking skills and writing and listening skills. An appendix includes other resources for further study, if desired.

7. Cullinan, Bernice E. (Editor). *Children's Literature in The Reading Program.* Newark, Delaware, International Reading Association, 1988.

   Many outstanding authorities in the field of children's literature have contributed chapters to this new book. There are numerous illustrations and specially designed sections to, acquaint the reader with specific teaching ideas. The many suggestions for utilizing certain books in the classroom reading program make this a very valuable source of information for *all* elementary teachers.

8. Cushenbery, Donald C. *Directing An Effective Language Arts Program For Your Students.* Springfield, Charles C Thomas, Publisher, 1986.

   Many important topics are discussed in this volume including the factors related to language development, evaluating language arts, and classroom organizational strategies for helping to insure maximum growth in reading, speaking, writing, and listening. The practical teaching procedures outlined for each elementary learning level make this a very valuable source for any instructor. The appendices contain useful information relating to instructional materials, tests, and professional books.

9. Cushenbery, Donald C. *Reading Instruction For The Gifted.* Springfield, Charles C Thomas, Publisher, 1987.

   The basic topics relating to the construction and implementation of a reading program for the gifted are discussed in detail in this volume. The reader is provided with many practical suggestions for identifying the gifted; building appropriate curricula for primary, intermediate, and secondary students; and evaluating the reading skill development levels of all learners.

10. Duffy, Gerald G. and Laura R. Roehler. *Improving Classroom Reading Instruction: A Decision-Making Approach.* New York, Random House, 1989.

    This important volume is designed for use with preservice students for helping them become professional teachers of reading. The 22 chapters are not separate and isolated but are presented in a cumulative manner, each succeeding chapter uses information from previous chapters as a starting point. Important learning devices include advance organizers; chapter headings and subheadings; figures, tables, and examples; vocabulary aids; and chapter summaries.

11. Ekwall, Eldon E. and James L. Shanker. *Teaching Reading In The Elementary School* (Second Edition). Columbus, Merrill Publishing Company, 1989.

    This book is about teaching developmental reading in the elementary school and is designed primarily as a reading methods book. The 13 chapters in the volume are devoted to all of the fundamental issues related to reading instruction such as the major approaches to reading, readiness, word attack, comprehension, and children with special reading needs. The appendices section is particularly valuable since it includes copies of various informal tests that can be used by all teachers.

12. Flood, James. (Editor). *Understanding Reading Comprehension.* Newark, Delaware, International Reading Association, 1984.

In this volume the author has compiled the writings of some of the most prominent scholars in the areas of cognition, language, and the structure of prose, with one section of the book devoted to each of these topics.

13. Garner, Ruth. *Metacognition and Reading Comprehension.* Norwood, New Jersey, Ablex Publishing Company, 1987.

Cognitive skills do not develop in a vacuum. This book is one in a series — Cognition and Literacy — which integrates cognitive processes, social context, and instruction. The ultimate goal of this series is to present research that may improve literacy acquisition by both children and adults. In this volume, basic research findings are examined from both methodological and developmental perspectives, and classroom strategies are suggested.

14. Goodman, Ken. *What's Whole In Language?* Portsmouth, New Hampshire, Heinemann Educational Books, 1986.

This valuable publication contains significant information relating to such significant issues as the what and why of language, the whole language view, and the teacher's role in building an effective whole language program. The sections are easy to read and the suggestions can be implemented easily by any elementary teacher. It is one of the best parent/teacher guides to children's learning that is available today.

15. Goodman, Kenneth S., Yetta M. Goodman, and Wendy J. Hood. (Editors). *The Whole Language Evaluation Book.* Portsmouth, New Hampshire, Heinemann Educational Books, 1989.

The 22 special articles in this paperback edition deal with all of the major issues concerned with the evaluation procedures to be used in a whole language program. The practical easy-to-understand strategies can be employed at all learning levels by teachers of little or much experience. The section relating to secondary and adult learners is extremely valuable since it directly correlated with second-language students.

16. Gould, Tony S. *The Right Start: A Practical Guide for Teaching Reading Readiness and Reading.* Cambridge, Massachusetts, Educators Publishing Service, 1988.

Since 1965 the author has developed a highly successful method of reading called Structural Reading. The twelve chapters are devoted to a detailed description of her method along with numerous suggestions and strategies for helping 2 and 3 year olds build readiness activities. The book should prove to be helpful to both parents and teachers in working with young children to prepare for the reading process.

17. Hancock, Joelie and Susan Hill (Editors). *Literature-Based Reading Programs at Work.* Portsmouth, New Hampshire, Heinemann Educational Books, 1987.

This is a book about change, specifically about teachers, administrators, specialists, and parents making the change from a basal-based reading program to a literature-based reading program. It is a book about beliefs, about teachers' questions and answers, and about problems and solutions. Detailed explanations regarding all phases of constructing and implementing a literature-based reading program are included.

18. Johnson, Marjorie Seddon, Roy A. Kress, and John J. Pikulski. *Informal Reading Inventories* (2nd Edition). Newark, Delaware, International Reading Association, 1987.

This is one of a number of helpful books in IRA's Reading Aids Series which can be utilized by the secondary classroom teacher who has had no formal reading background. The informal reading inventory helps to "fit" the student with the reading materials presented.

19. Landsberg, Michele. *Reading For The Love of It: Best Books for Young Readers.* New York, Prentice-Hall, 1987.

The author, an award-winning journalist, has had much experience with hundreds of children's books. The book has two major sections—the first designed to develop background information and provide the teacher or parent with appropriate guidelines for choosing the right books. The second major part of the book contains about 400 annotations of fictional books for pupils from ages 5–15.

20. McNeil, John D. *Reading Comprehension—New Directions for Classroom Practice.* Dallas, Scott, Foresman and Company, 1984.

Teaching reading comprehension and how new theory and research have validated new methods of teaching are the primary concerns of this text. The book includes demonstrations of practical ways theory and practice can be combined.

21. Moore, David W., John E. Readence, and Robert J. Rickelman. *Prereading Activities for Content Area Reading and Learning.* (2nd Edition). Newark, Delaware, International Reading Association, 1988.

The authors describe a large number of prereading activities and strategies designed to provide significant help for teachers in making many kinds of content reading both readable and understandable for learners. One of the important features of this new volume is a complete and thorough chapter on the background and use of writing in the content subjects.

22. Nagy, William E. *Teaching Vocabulary To Improve Reading Comprehension.* Newark, Delaware, International Reading Association, 1988.

Nagy makes a valiant attempt to translate research into classroom practice by suggesting to teachers how they can use vocabulary teaching procedures to upgrade comprehension skill development. The activities involving prereading strategies are most valuable and interesting. Elementary classroom teachers and all reading specialists who work with students in the upper grades will find this book especially helpful.

23. Pavlok, Stephen A. *Classroom Activities for Correcting Specific Reading Problems.* West Nyack, New York, Parker Publishing Company, 1985.

This book contains over 230 sequentially organized activities, games, and exercises to correct specific skill weaknesses in the areas of phonic analysis, structural analysis, comprehension, and oral reading, as well as "survival" reading skills.

24. Readence, John E., Thomas W. Bean and R. Scott Baldwin. *Content Area Reading: An Integrated Approach.* Dubuque, Iowa, Kendall/Hunt Publishing Company, 1981.

    This text is designed to make subject matter specialists better teachers of their content, rather than teachers of reading. Thus, it provides teachers with a comprehensive examination of content area reading.

25. Reed, Arthea J.S. *Comics To Classics: A Parents Guide for Teens and Preteens.* Newark, Delaware, International Reading Association, 1988.

    This new source is invaluable for *both* parents and elementary teachers since it contains a booklist that briefly describes over 300 books for young people. Each of the listings contains a brief plot summary, a guide to age range, and elements of the book that may be of special interest. The ideas in Reed's books are targeted to reach reluctant readers to give books a place in their lives.

26. Smith, Carl B. and Peggy Gordon Elliot. *Reading Activities for Middle and Secondary Schools* (2nd Edition). New York, Teachers College Press, 1986.

    This is an activity book, not a theory book. It is designed to provide samples and models to follow in developing activities that will help students to read more effectively. It's organization as a handbook will help teachers quickly see how the material can be used in content areas.

27. Stoodt, Barbara D. *Reading Instruction* (Second Edition). New York, Harper and Row, Publishers, 1989.

    This outstanding volume is divided into four parts and contains 11 chapters and three appendices sections. The present edition emphasizes whole language and combining whole language with other approaches. Thinking skills and higher-order thinking skills are emphasized. Specific suggestions and models for teaching are included. The organizational pattern of the material is easy to follow and understand.

28. Taylor, Barbara, Larry A. Harris, and L. David Pearson. *Reading Difficulties: Instruction and Assessment.* New York, Random House, 1988.

    The authors have divided this important new source into four sections (1) the fundamentals of reading difficulties; (2) instruction and assessment for low-achieving readers; (3) traditional approaches to reading difficulties; and (4) remedial programs. The chapter organizer consists of chapter summaries, activities, notes, and suggested readings make this volume of the most authoritative, easy-to-read book available to teachers.

29. Thompson, Richard A. (Editor). *Classroom Reading Instruction.* Dubuque, Iowa, Kendall/Hunt Publishing Company, 1989.

    The more than 30 contributors to this new volume are members of the Organization of Teacher Educators in Reading. Many diverse, valuable topics are explored in the 31 chapters. Some of them are individualized reading; culturally and linguistically different learners; teaching and remediating sight word vocabulary; increasing reading rates; and improving comprehension ability. The paperback edition is especially designed to be used as a supplemental source for a reading methods course.

30. Twining, James E. *Reading and Thinking: A Process Approach.* New York, Holt, Rinehart and Winston, 1985.

The purpose of this book is to provide a practical methodology for the active involvement of the reader in the development and application of reading strategies. Chapters include Understanding Main Ideas, Employing Prior Knowledge, Vocabulary Strategies, Asking Questions, Reading Textbooks, Learning and Memory, and Taking Examinations.

31. Vacca, Richard T. and Jo Anne L. Vacca. *Content Area Reading.* (Third Edition). Glenview, Illinois, Scott, Foresman and Company, 1989.

The newly revised chapters in this important new volume include valuable information relating to such significant topics as study skills and how to recognize the attributes of chapter organization. Building background of knowledge for each content subject is an important topic discussed. Middle grade teachers will find the well written suggestions to be very useful in helping individual pupils to build maximum reading skills levels.

32. Wilson, Robert M. and Craig J. Cleland. *Diagnostic and Remedial Reading For Classrooms and Clinics* (Sixth Edition). Columbus, Merrill Publishing Company, 1989.

The new edition of this classic text contains several chapters that should be interesting and valuable for all elementary teachers. Two entirely new chapters have been added: one on uses and interpretation of standardized tests, and one on microcomputer and closed-caption television technologies. Additional topics include comprehension strategies, English as a second language, metacognition, and reading/writing connections.

33. Zintz, Miles and Z. R. Maggart. *Corrective Reading.* (5th Edition). Dubuque, Iowa, William C. Brown Publishers, 1986.

The authors present an overview of the reading process with an emphasis on the diagnostic teaching of reading. Pre-assessment, teaching, then post-assessment is described and throughout the book, the emphasis is on *corrective* teaching.

# Appendix C

# LIST OF PUBLISHERS AND THEIR ADDRESSES

Addison-Wesley Publishing Company, Inc. Jacob Way, Reading, Massachusetts 01867

Aims Instructional Media, Inc., 626 Justin Avenue, Glendale, California 91201

Alfred Higgins Productions, 9100 Sunset Boulevard, Los Angeles, California 90069

Alfred A. Knopf, Inc. 201 East 50th Street, New York, New York, 10022

Allyn and Bacon, 470 Atlantic Avenue, Boston, Massachusetts 02210

American Educational Computer, Inc. 2450 Embarcadero Way, Palo Alto, California 94303

American Guidance Service, Publisher's Building, P.O. Box 99, Circle Pines, Minnesota 55014-1796

American Health Partners, 80 Fifth Avenue, New York, New York 10011

Antioch Review, Inc., P.O. Box 148, Yellow Springs, Ohio 45387

Aspen Systems Corporation, 1600 Research Boulevard, Rockville, Maryland 20850

Astromedia Corp., 625 East St. Paul Avenue, Box 92788, Milwaukee, Wisconsin 53202

Audio-Visual Research Company, P.O. Box 71, Waseca, Minnesota 56093

A. V. Concepts Corporation, 30 Montauk Boulevard, Oakdale, New York 11769

Barnell Loft, Ltd., 958 Church Street, Baldwin, New York 11510

Benjamin Franklin Literary & Medical Society, Inc., 1100 Waterway Boulevard, Box 567, Indianapolis, Indiana 46206

Boy Scouts of America, Inc., 1325 Walnut Hill Lane, Irving, Texas 75602

Borg-Warner Educational System, 600 West University Drive, Arlington Heights, Illinois 60004

BFA Educational Media, P.O. Box 1795, 2211 Michigan Avenue, Santa Monica, California 90406

Brain Bank, Inc., P.O. Box 1708, Greenville, Texas 75401

Brigham Young University, Media Marketing, Provo, Utah 84602

William C. Brown Company, 2460 Kerper Boulevard, Dubuque, Iowa 52001

California Test Bureau, McGraw-Hill, Del Monte Research Park, Monterey, California 93940

Camp Fire, Inc., 4601 Madison Avenue, Kansas City, Missouri 64112

Cardinal Software, 13646 Jefferson Davis Highway, Woodbridge, Virginia 22191

Charles Merrill Publishing Company, 1300 Alum Creek Drive, Columbus, Ohio 43216

Charles C Thomas, Publisher, 2600 South First Street, Springfield, Illinois 62794

Child Life, 1100 Waterway Boulevard, 567B, Indianapolis, Indiana 46202

Children's Television Workshop, One Lincoln Plaza, New York, New York 10023

Cobblestone Publishing, Inc., 20 Grove Street, Peterborough, New Hampshire 03458

College Entrance Examination Board, 888 Seventh Avenue, New York, New York 10106

Committee on Diagnostic Reading Tests, Mountain Home, North Carolina 28758

Computer Assisted Instruction, Inc. 6115 28th Street, S.E., Grand Rapids, Michigan 45506

Computer Courseware Company, 2118 South Grand Avenue, Santa Ana, California 92705

Computer Curriculum Corporation, 1070 Arastradero Road, P.O. Box 10080, Palo Alto, California 94303

Computer Island, 227 Hampton Green, Staten Island, New York 10312

Consumers Union of U.S. Inc., 256 Washington Street, Mt. Vernon, New York 10553

The Continental Press, Inc., Elizabethtown, Pennsylvania 17022

Coronet Films and Video, 108 Wilmot Road, Deerfield, Illinois 60015

Creative Curriculum, Inc./Computer Courseware, Inc.

Crestwood House, Highway 66 South, Box 3427, Mankato, Minnesota 56002-3427

Croft, Inc. 4601 York Road, Baltimore, Maryland 21212

Curriculum Associates, Inc. 5 Esquire Road, North Billerica, Massachusetts 01821

Data Command of Imperial International Learning Corp., P.O. Box 272, Fairfield, Ohio 45014

Davis Readers Group, 380 Lexington Avenue, New York, New York 10017

Developmental Learning Materials, 7440 Natchez Avenue, Niles, Illinois 60648

Walt Disney Educational Media Company, 500 South Buena Vista Street, Burbank, California 91521

DLM Teaching Resources, P.O. Box 4000, One DLM Park, Allen, Texas 75002

DOK Publishers, 71 Radcliffe Road, Buffalo, New York 14214

Dushkin Publishing Group, Inc., Sluice Dock, Guilford, Connecticut 06437

Economy Company Individualized Instruction Incorporated, P.O. Box 25308, 1901 North Walnut, Oklahoma City, Oklahoma 73125

Edmark Corporation, P.O. Box 3903, Bellevue, Washington 98009

Education Activities, Inc., Box 392, Freeport, New York 11520

Educational Developmental Laboratories, Inc., 1221 Avenue of the Americas, New York, New York 10020

Educational Reading Services, 320 State Highway 17, Mahwah, New Jersey 07430

Educators Publishing Service, Inc., 75 Moulton Street, Cambridge, Massachusetts 02238

Educulture, Inc., One Dubuque Plaza, Suite 730, Dubuque, Iowa 52001

EMC Publishing Changing Times Education Service, 180 East Sixth Street, Saint Paul, Minnesota 60607

ESP, Inc., Box 5037, Jonesboro, Arkansas 72403

Fancy Publications, Inc., Box 4030, San Clemente, California 92672

Fandom Unlimited Enterprises, Box 70868, Sunnyvale, California 94069

Fearon Teacher Aids, 19 Davis Drive, Belmont, California 94002

Follett Library Book Co., 4506 Northwest Highway, Crystal Lake, Illinois 60014

Four Winds Press: (A division of Scholastic), 906 Sylvan Avenue, Englewood Cliffs, New Jersey 07632

Gallent Charger Publications, 34249 Camino Capistrano, Box H. Capistrano Beach, California 92624

Garrard Publishing Company, 1607 North Market Street, P.O. Box A, Champaign, Illinois 61820

GCT Publishing Co., Inc., Box 6448, Mobile, Alabama 36660

Ginn Company, P.O. Box 2649, 1250 Fairwood Avenue, Columbus, Ohio 43216

Good Apple, Inc., USPS 301-80, Box 299, Carthage, Illinois 62321

Gruner & Jahr USA Publishing, 685 Third Avenue, New York, New York 10017

Harper and Row, Inc., 10 East 53rd Street, New York, New York 10022

Hartley Courseware, Inc., 133 Bridge Street, Box 419, Dimondale, Michigan 48821

Hearst Corp., 959 Eighth Avenue, New York, New York 10021

D.C. Heath and Company, 125 Spring Street, Lexington, Massachusetts 02173

Highlights for Children, Box 269, Columbus, Ohio 43272

Holt, Rinehart, and Winston CBS, Inc., 383 Madison Avenue, New York, New York 10017

Houghton Mifflin Company, 1900 South Batavia Avenue, Geneva, Illinois 60134

Instructional Communications Technology, Inc., 10 Stepar Place, Huntington Station, New York 11746

Instructional Fair, Inc., P.O. Box 1650, Grand Rapids, Michigan 49501

The Instructor Publications, Inc. Instructor Books, 757 Third Avenue, New York, New York 10017

Intellectual Software, 798 North Avenue, Bridgeport, Connecticut 06606

Intercollegiate Video Clearinghouse, Inc., P.O. Drawer 33000R, Miami, Florida 33133

International Reading Association, 800 Barksdale Road, Newark, Delaware 19714

Jam Magazine/Ltd., 56 The Esplande, Ste. 202, Toronto, Ontario M5E1A7 Canada

Jamestown Publishers, The Reading People, P.O. box 6743, Providence, Rhode Island 02940

J/C Enterprises, Inc., 4920 Mayflower Street, Cocoa, Florida 32927

Kiplinger Washington Editors, Inc., 1729 "H" Street N.W., Washington, D.C. 20006

Laidlaw Brothers. Thatcher and Madison, River Forest, Illinois 60305

The Learning Line, P.O. Box 1200, Palo Alto, California 94302

Learning Well, 200 South Service Road, Roslyn Heights, New York 11577

Learning Periodicals Group, 19 Davis Drive, Belmont, California 94002

Learning Research Associates, P.O. Box 39, Roslyn Heights, New York 11577

Light & Life Press, 999 College Avenue, Winona Lake, Indiana 46590

Little, Brown and Company, 34 Beacon Street, Boston, Massachusetts 02106

Longman, Inc., 19 West 44th Street, New York, New York 10036

MacMillan Publishing Company, Inc., 866 Third Avenue, New York, New York 10022

Macmillan Education Ltd., Houndsmills, Basingstoke, Hampshire RG21 2XS, U.K.

Massachusetts Audubon Society, South Great Road, Lincoln, Massachusetts 01773

McGraw-Hill Book Company, 1221 Avenue of the Americas, New York, New York 10016

Charles E. Merrill Company, 1300 Alum Creek Drive, Columbus, Ohio 43216

Micro School Programs, 3647 Stone Way North, Seattle, Washington 98103

Micrograms, Inc., P.O. Box 2146, Loves Park, Illinois 61130

Micropower and Light Company, 12820 Hillcrest Road, Suite 219, Dallas, Texas 75230

Midwest Publications, P.O. Box 448, Pacific Grove, California 93950

Milliken, 1100 Research Boulevard, P.O. Box 21579, St. Louis, Missouri 63132

Milton Bradley, 443 Shaker Road, East Longmeadow, Massachusetts 01028

Modern Curriculum Press, 13900 Prospect Road, Cleveland, Ohio 44136

Modulearn, Inc., P.O. Box 667, San Juan Capistrano, California 92693

Mutual Aid, 1953½ Hillhurst Avenue, Los Angeles, California 90027

National Association of State Boards of Education, 444 North Capitol Street N.W., Washington, D.C. 20001

National Audubon Society, 950 Third Avenue, New York, New York 10022

National Geographic Society, 17th and M Street, N.W., Washington, D.C. 20036

National Wildlife Federation, Inc., 1412 Sixteenth Street N.W., Washington, D.C. 20036

New York Zoological Society, 185th Street and Southern Boulevard, Bronx, New York 10460

Nystrom Division of Carnation Co., 33033 Elston Avenue, Chicago, Illinois 60618

Open Court Publishing, P.O. Box 100, LaSalle, Illinois 61301

Opportunities for Learning, Inc., 8950 Lurline Avenue, Dept. W, Chatsworth, California 91311

Orange Cherry Media, 7 Delano Drive, Bedford Hills, Connecticut 06156

Pendulum Press, Inc., Saw Mill Road, West Haven, Connecticut 06516

Prentice-Hall, Educational Book Division, Englewood Cliffs, New Jersey 07632

Psychological Corporation, 7500 Old Oak Boulevard, Cleveland, Ohio 44130

Psychotechnics, Inc., 1900 Pickwick Avenue, Glenview, Illinois 60025

Publishers Test Service, 2500 Garden Road, Monterey, California 93940-5380

Radio Shack/Tandy Corporation, Fort Worth, Texas 76102

Rand McNally College Publishing Company, Box 7600, Chicago, Illinois 60680

Random House, School Division, 400 Hahn Road, Westminster, Massachusetts 21157

Reader's Digest Services, Inc., Educational Division, Pleasantville, New York 10570

Reading Institute, 116 Newbury Street, Boston, Massachusetts 02116

Reading Laboratory, Inc., 55 Day Street, South Norwalk, Connecticut 06854

R/C Modeler Corp., 144 West Sierra Madre Boulevard, Sierra Madre, California 91024

The Riverside Publishing Company, 8420 Bryn Mawr Avenue, Chicago, Illinois 60631

The Saturday Evening Post Co., 100 Waterway Boulevard, Box 567B, Indianapolis, Indiana 46202

Scholastic, Inc., 1290 Wall Street West, Lyndhurst, New Jersey 07071

Scienceland, 501 Fifth Avenue, New York, New York 10017

Scholastic, Inc., 904 Sylvan Avenue, Englewood Cliffs, New York 07632

Science Research Associates, Inc., 259 East Erie Street, Chicago, Illinois 60611

Scott, Foresman and Company, 1900 East Lake Avenue, Glenview, Illinois 60025

Sigma XI, The Scientific Research Society, 345 Whitney Avenue, New Haven, Connecticut 06511

Smithsonian Institution, 900 Jefferson Drive, Washington, D.C. 20560

Softside/Software, 10 Northern Boulevard, Amherst, New Hampshire 03031-2312

Special Learning Corporation, Guilford, Connecticut 06437

Spinnaker Press, Inc., Pickering Wharf, Salem, Massachusetts 01970

Society for Visual Education, Inc., 1345 Diversey Parkway, Chicago, Illinois 60614

Steck-Vaughn Company, P.O. Box 2028, Austin, Texas 78768

Sunburst Communications, Room VH-5, 39 Washington Avenue, Pleasantville, New York 10570

Teachers College Press, P.O. Box 1540, Hagerstown, Maryland 21740

T.F.H. Publications, Inc., 211 West Sylvania Avenue, Neptune City, New Jersey 07753

Troll Associates, 320 State Highway 17, Mahwah, New Jersey 07430

Two Fathoms Publishing, 2021 Brunswick Street, Suite 209B, Halifax, NS B3K 2Y5 Canada

Unity School of Christianity, Unity Village, Missouri 64065

U.S. Scholastic, Inc., 730 Broadway, New York, New York 10003

Universal Systems for Education, Inc., 195 Bonhomme Street, Hackensack, New Jersey 07602

D. Van Nostrand Company, 450 West 33rd Street, New York, New York 10001

John Wiley and Sons, Inc., 605 Third Avenue, New York, New York 10016

Winston Press, 25 Groveland Terrace, Minneapolis, Minnesota 55403

The Wright Group, 7620 Miramar Road, Suite 4200, San Diego, California 92126

Wise Owl Workshop, 1168 Avenue de las Palmas, Livermore, California 94550

World Poetry, Inc., 1616 Walnut, Room 405, Philadelphia, Pennsylvania 19103

Young Naturalist Foundation, 51 Front Street, E, Toronto, Ontario M5E1B3, Canada

Zaner-Bloser, P.O. Box 16764, Columbus, Ohio 43216-6764

Ziff Davis Publishing, 1 Park Avenue, New York, New York 10016

# AUTHOR INDEX

## A

Allard, Harry, 44
Alexander, J. Estelle, 141
Andersen, Dennis R., 17
Anderson, Richard, 10
Aulls, Mark W. 125, 141

## B

Baldwin, R. Scott, 145
Barr, Rebecca, 141
Baumann, Jane F., 141
Bean, Thomas W., 145
Berglund, Roberta L., 52
Bernagozzi, Tom, 112, 114
Bitzer, Donald, 28
Bond, Guy M., 78, 86
Burns, Paul C., 16, 37
Butterfield, Dennie, 35, 37

## C

Carbo, Marie, 20, 36
Carter, Susan H., 52
Chernoff, Loren, 114
Cheyney, Arnold B., 142
Clary, Linda Mixon, 23, 36, 70, 85
Cleland, Craig J., 76, 86, 146
Coon, George E. 52
Craddock, Sonja, 53
Cullinan, Bernice E., 142
Cunningham, Patricia M., 16
Cushenbery, Donald C., 86, 89, 102, 125, 142

## D

De Vries, David, 111
Dishon, Dee, 113

Duffy, Gerald G., 86, 97, 102, 142
Durkin, Dolores, 67, 102, 118, 125

## E

Eanet, Marilyn, 102
Ekwall, Eldon E., 142
Eldredge, J. Lloyd, 35, 37
Elliot, Peggy Gordon, 145

## F

Falcon, Susan Claire, 59, 67
Farr, Roger, 66, 67
Farris, Pamela J. 52
Feiertag, Judy, 114
Finn, Patrick J. 16, 66
Flood, James, 143
Futrell, Mary, 75

## G

Garner, Ruth, 143
Geoffrion, Leo D., 28, 37
Geoffrion, Olga P. 28, 37
Goddard, Connie Heaton, 17
Good, Thomas L., 36
Goodman, Ken, 40, 52, 143
Goodman, Yetta M., 143
Gould, Tony S., 143
Gray, Mary Jane, 70, 85
Gronlund, Norman E., 125
Gunderson, Lee, 46, 47, 52

## H

Hafner, Lawrence E., 17
Halpern, Honey, 53
Hancock, Joelie, 114, 143
Harker, John, 16

153

# SUBJECT INDEX